Senior Leaders
Cookbook

Recipes and Memories from our Kitchen Table to Yours

This book is dedicated to the many women and men
who prepare the food and share the traditions that nurture us
— body, mind and soul.

Senior Leaders, Inc.
Memphis, Tennessee

Proceeds from the sale of the
Senior Leaders Cookbook:
Recipes and Memories From Our Kitchen Table To Yours
will solely benefit the programs of Senior Leaders, Inc.

Cookbook Committee Chair: Jennie Morring

Published by Senior Leaders, Inc.
2670 Union Avenue Extended, Suite 1000
Memphis, TN 38112
901-324-3299

Editor: Bridget Ciaramitaro
Publication Manager: Heather Baugus

This cookbook is a collection of favorite recipes from our friends, families and supporters. Many have been passed down through generations and are now being passed on to you. They are not necessarily original recipes. Liberties have been taken to ensure consistency of form.

Printed in the USA by
WIMMER
The Wimmer Companies
Memphis
1-800-548-2537

We would like to thank our Sponsors

Sous Chef $5,000 – $9,999
The H.W. Durham Foundation
Lorraine and Herb Kaufman

Sommelier $3,000 – $4,999
The Aging Commission of the Mid-South

Pastry Chef $1,000 – $2,999
Deweese & Associates
in memory of Pearl L. Watson
– Dr. Robert Burns and Dr. Linda Nichols
in honor of Martha Nichols

Maitre de $500 – $999
– Ciaramitaro and Associates
– East Memphis LIFE Chapter
in memory of Nelda Grimes
– Elnora Farwell LIFE Chapter
in memory of Elnora Farwell
– Friends of Chris Glass
in memory of Chris Glass

"Senior Leaders
brings together people from many diverse
backgrounds who may have previously led parallel lives."

~ Community Leader

After years of planning and endless hours of rumbling tummies while reading through so many delicious recipes, we are finally able to share them with you. In this book, you will find far more than a wide array of tasty delectables. You will find a stage from which you will hear the stories of traditions and moments past from seniors, community leaders, friends and supporters. So whether you are a cook or a cookbook collector, you will love this opportunity to glance into the busy kitchens and warm hearts of our contributors. It may even inspire you to compile your own collection of favorite recipes and memories to be handed down to friends and family!

Enjoy!

Jennie Morring
Cookbook Committee Chair
Memphis, Tennessee

Our Mission

The mission of Senior Leaders, Inc. is to empower seniors to remain independent and to be leaders in meeting diverse needs in the community.

Our Programs

LEADERSHIP FOR AN INDEPENDENT FUTURE (LIFE)

LIFE prepares seniors with the attitude, skills, motivation and knowledge needed to remain independent and to be leaders of their own lives and leaders in their community. These classes address the growing desire of seniors to remain at home for as long as possible. This innovative, empowerment program has successfully graduated over 1000 seniors in Memphis, Shelby County and beyond.

AGE STAGE

The Age Stage Theatre Troupe reaches diverse audiences with vital information about aging through impromptu and interactive productions. This program is dedicated to raising awareness of issues relevant to seniors, generating solutions to problems of aging and expanding seniors' appreciation of and participation in the arts. Over 1300 seniors, their families and professionals participate each year throughout the Mid-South.

SENIOR VOICES

Senior Voices is a video and multimedia production program that creates, preserves and distributes educational and motivational materials for and about seniors. Since 1998, four Senior Voices productions have received national awards: *No Place I'd Rather Be: Long Term Care Choices in Tennessee; The Best Is Yet To Be; Aging Aren't We All;* and *Healthy Aging.* Thousands of seniors, families, service providers and others have been inspired by these videos that give a voice to seniors themselves as they directly experience the challenges and opportunities of aging. Write or call Senior Leaders, Inc. for a list of videos and audiotapes available for purchase.

Recipe for Happiness

2 heaping cups of patience
2 handfuls of generosity
1 heart full of love
1 head full of understanding
Dash of laughter

Sprinkle generously with kindness. Add plenty of faith. Mix well. Spread over a period of a lifetime and serve everybody you meet. Be a blessing to others and you'll always reap what you sow.

Helen Lockhart, Class of 1995

Cookbook Committee

Without the enthusiasm of all of those involved, this book would have not been possible. We would like to acknowledge the hard work and dedication of those individuals who offered so much of their time and talent so that this book could be shared with others.

Jennie Morring, Chair	Nelda Grimes	Desiree Robinson
Heather Baugus	Lorraine Kaufman	Merle Smith
Marilyn Baugus	Mattie Lindsey	Gail Spake
Bridget Ciaramitaro	Lillie Nelson	David Williams
Symeria Clemons	Linda Nichols	Gary Witt
Evelyn Cornelius	Robert McFalls	

Table of Contents

Recipes from the
Tables of Community Leaders

No matter how old you are, life is still beautiful.

*Thanks to the following community leaders
who have shared their delicious recipes and stories in support
of our efforts to empower seniors.*

Bev Johnson

Mary and Joe Scheuner

Harry Shaw

Drs. Robert Burns and Linda Nichols

Bill Ramsey

Congressman Harold Ford, Jr.

Ray and Desiree Robinson

William L. Gibbons

Renee Smith

Ken Hall

Robert McFalls

Bobby Ojay

Fred "Hollywood" Moore

Joyce Cobb

Reverend Dr. and Mrs. Fred Lofton

Dave Brown

Earl Randall

Marybeth Conley

Nelly Galloway Shearer

Tommie Cervetti

Annie McDaniel

Maybell Danner's Hot Water Cornbread

1	cup self-rising cornmeal	Cold water
1	teaspoon all-purpose	Canola oil
	flour, optional	

In a heat safe mixing bowl, mix together meal and flour. Set aside. Fill a black cast iron skillet almost completely with cold water and bring to a boil. Pour boiling water into meal. Stir until the water cooks the meal and is thick. Add oil to skillet, completely covering bottom. Heat until hot. Make meal mixture into patties and place in hot oil. Cook until both sides are golden brown. Serve with butter or margarine while still hot. Now that's good, down-home southern eating!

Bev Johnson,
WDIA Radio Personality

My most fond memories of growing up were sitting at the kitchen table with my Grandmother, Mrs. Maybell Danner. As the young folks would say, my Grandmother was the Bomb! And a darn good cook. Her food was always tasty, and she didn't take a long time to prepare it. My Grandmother was a domestic worker, and I remember her off days being Thursday and Sunday. My sister and I would always wait for Thursdays because we knew we would have a great treat. But I guess my favorite meal from my Grandmother would be turnip greens with the bottoms, candied yams, neck bones, okra, black-eyed peas and Hot Water Cornbread. That was the best tasting stuff I had ever eaten, and especially when you loaded it with butter and it was served hot out of the skillet. I could just eat the bread by itself, and didn't have to have the other food. As a matter of fact, everyone loved my Grandmother's hot water cornbread, and now being the age of 47, friends from the neighborhood still talk about it. And if I do say so myself, I make the best hot water cornbread too. So here it is, Maybell Danner's Hot Water Cornbread.

Party Chopped Herring

12	ounces jarred herring fillet, not in cream sauce	3	ounces chopped pecans
10	ounces pineapple chunks, drained and chopped	1	hard red apple, cored and chopped in small pieces
½	medium red onion, finely chopped	¼	carrot, grated
		1	tablespoon mayonnaise
		6	ounces sour cream

Drain herring well on paper towels, blotting off all liquid. Chop in small pieces and blot again on fresh paper towels. Mix together all ingredients until moist, but not runny. Refrigerate until ready to serve.

Note: Flavor improves, so prepare 4 to 7 days in advance.

Yield: 60 servings

Mary and Joe Scheuner

My mother, Mary Tetreault Pusch, was a career woman in the days when fewer women chose that path. For 49 years, she was a dress designer in New York City. In 1948, she won a Coty Award - fashion's equivalent of the Oscar.

Due to the demands of her career, mother did not cook family meals. She did, however, entertain and she did so lavishly. My earliest experiences in the kitchen were as her helper, chopping, slicing, measuring and stirring under her direction. These times together taught me more than the rudiments of cooking. My mother taught me how to entertain, how to prepare everything possible in advance in order to have a wonderful time at your own party. Every time I serve one of her specialties, I get lots of compliments from my guests, and I enjoy wonderful memories of those times as her assistant.

Rave Review Rice Pilaf

1	can beef bouillon	1	can mushrooms, drained
1	can onion soup	1	cup rice, not instant
¾	stick margarine		

Combine all ingredients. Pour into baking dish and bake at 350 degrees uncovered for 1 hour.

Note: This is a family recipe and goes great with any meat!

Harry Shaw, President
United Way of the Mid-South

Deep Dish Spinach Pizza

DOUGH

1	packet yeast	1	cup water
½	teaspoon granulated sugar	2½	cups all-purpose flour
		1	egg, room temperature

SAUCE

1-2	cloves garlic	2	(28 ounce) cans
1	medium onion, chopped		tomatoes, chopped
2	tablespoons olive oil		Oregano to taste

TOPPING

2	(10 ounce) boxes frozen, chopped spinach, defrosted and squeezed dry	12	ounces mozzarella Romano, optional Red pepper, optional

Dissolve yeast and sugar in warm water and allow to sit until foamy, approximately 5 minutes. In a large bowl, put in flour and add yeast mixture. Add egg. Mix. Knead by hand or with dough hook until dough is slightly tacky to touch. Let dough rise in warm place until double in size. Sauté garlic and onion in olive oil until soft. Add tomatoes and simmer until thick and juice is boiled off, approximately 30 minutes. Set aside. Pat dough into one 12 inch circle and place in oiled pizza pan. Top with spinach, cheese and then sauce. Sprinkle with oregano. Bake at 425 degrees for 20 minutes. Top with Romano and red pepper if desired before serving.

Dr. Robert Burns and Dr. Linda Nichols
Honorary Class of 2000 and 1996

Pan Seared Rib-Eye

1 boneless rib-eye steak 1½ inch thick Canola oil or olive oil	Kosher salt and ground black pepper to taste

Place 10 to 12 inch cast iron skillet in oven and heat to 500 degrees. Bring steak to room temperature. When oven reaches temperature, remove skillet from oven and place on range over high heat. Coat steak lightly with oil and season both sides with a generous pinch of salt. Grind on black pepper to taste. Immediately place steak in middle of hot, dry pan. Cook 30 seconds without moving. Turn with tongs and cook another 30 seconds. Then put the pan back in the oven for 2 minutes. Flip steak and cook for another 2 minutes. This is timed for medium rare steaks. Add up to 3 minutes per side as desired. Remove steak from pan, cover loosely with foil, and rest for 2 minutes. Serve whole or slice thin.

Note: If you prefer well done or crispy steak, cook it longer on top of stove and in oven.

Yield: 1 to 2 servings

Bill Ramsey
Assistant District Attorney

Sweet Potato Pie

4 medium sweet potatoes	1½ teaspoons Watkins vanilla flavor
1 stick butter or margarine	1 small can Pet evaporated milk
1 cup granulated sugar	1 (9 inch) pie crust
3 eggs	
¼ teaspoon nutmeg	

Peel and slice potatoes. Boil until tender. Drain and place in mixing bowl. Add butter to potatoes and stir until melted. Add other ingredients and mix well. Pour mixture into pie crust and bake at 350 degrees for 30 to 35 minutes.

Congressman Harold Ford, Jr.

Coffee-Laced Barbecue Sauce

1 cup ketchup	¼ stick margarine,
⅓ cup hot sauce	optional
⅓ cup Worcestershire	2 tablespoons lemon juice
sauce	1 teaspoon instant coffee
⅓ cup brown sugar, honey	1 tablespoon cider
or molasses	vinegar

Mix all ingredients in a saucepan. Simmer for 30 to 40 minutes.

Ray and Desiree Robinson, Owners
Cozy Corner Restaurant

Velveeta Cheese Fudge

1 pound Velveeta Cheese,	4 pounds sugar
chopped into 2 inch	¾ cup cocoa
cubes	½ teaspoon salt
1 pound margarine,	2 tablespoons vanilla
chopped into 2 inch	1 cup chopped nuts
cubes	

Put cheese and margarine into heavy saucepan over medium heat. Stir until completely melted, and then beat well. Set aside until slightly cool. In a large pot or dish pan, mix sugar, cocoa and salt. Make a well in center of dry mixture. Pour cheese mixture into center of dry ingredients. Add vanilla and mix well with hands. Mix in nuts. Divide mixture in half. Grease two 9 x 13 x 3 inch pans. Press mixture into pans. Place in refrigerator until hard. Cut into squares.

Yield: 6 pounds

Annie McDaniel, Friend of Senior Leaders
Mississippi River Story Teller

Bodacious Banana

1	box banana cake mix	1	can whipped cream
1	box instant banana pudding	1	banana, sliced
1	(8 ounce) package cream cheese		Dash nutmeg

Prepare banana cake as directed. While cake is baking, prepare pudding. Cut chunks of cream cheese into pudding to thicken. If you use all of the cream cheese, you may wish to add a dash of milk. Refrigerate pudding. Remove cake from oven and cut into squares. Dollop pudding generously onto cake squares, cover with whipped cream, arrange banana slices on tops and dust with nutmeg.

Ken Hall
Founder and Executive Director of
Hands On Memphis

Crab Cheese Ball

1	(8 ounce) package cream cheese (not low fat)		Chopped onion to taste
		$\frac{1}{8}$	teaspoon hot sauce
		$\frac{1}{8}$	teaspoon soy sauce
1	can crabmeat, drained		Chopped nuts or
1	teaspoon lemon juice		Paprika
$\frac{1}{2}$	teaspoon garlic salt		

Mix together first 7 ingredients with a fork until mixture is somewhat smooth. Roll mixture into a ball. Roll in chopped nuts or sprinkle with Paprika. Serve with crackers.

Renee Smith
Founder and President
of Caring Companions

Spinach Artichoke Casserole

2 (10 ounce) packages frozen chopped spinach	½ teaspoon salt
	½ teaspoon white pepper
	Dash red pepper
½ cup chopped onion	½ cup mozzarella cheese
¼ cup butter, melted	2 (14 ounce) cans artichoke hearts, drained and chopped
3-4 ounces cream cheese	
½ cup sour cream	
¼ cup Parmesan cheese, grated	2 tablespoons Parmesan cheese

Cook and drain spinach. Set aside. In a large skillet, sauté onion in butter. Add cream cheese, cooking until melted. Add spinach, sour cream, ¼ cup Parmesan cheese, salt, white pepper, red pepper and mozzarella cheese. Fold artichokes into spinach mixture. Pour into greased 3 inch baking dish. Sprinkle with remaining Parmesan cheese. Bake at 350 degrees for 25 to 30 minutes.

Yield: 8 servings

Robert McFalls, Executive Director
Aging Commission of the Mid-South

This recipe has been passed from kitchen to kitchen of many friends and acquaintances. Sharing makes cooking all the more enjoyable!

Bobby Ojay's Anytime Drink

½ cantaloupe, cut into small pieces	½ cup raspberry yogurt
	8 pieces crystallized ginger
1 banana	1 cup orange juice, or more to taste
8 strawberries, fresh or frozen	
	1½ cups vanilla soy protein

Mix all ingredients in a blender for about 45 seconds. Pour into a glass and enjoy!

Bobby Ojay, WDIA Radio Personality

I drink this as breakfast and it keeps me full until around lunch, but you can drink it anytime you wish!

Geneva's Special Baked Corn

2	eggs, beaten	½	cup melted butter
1	can creamed corn	1	cup boxed cornbread
1	can whole kernel corn		mix
1	cup sour cream	8-10	saltine crackers
⅓	cup granulated sugar	1	cup shredded cheese

Stir together eggs, corn, sour cream, sugar, butter and corn bread mix. Pour into greased 2-quart casserole or 9 x 11 inch baking dish. Mash or roll crackers fine. Sprinkle on top of corn mixture. Cover with shredded cheese. Bake at 325 degrees for 1 hour or until firm in center.

Fred "Hollywood" Moore
WDIA Radio Personality

A smile always comes to my face as I remember the many Thanksgiving dinners at my grandmother's house. Nana, as the family called her, could take the simplest dish and make it so special as she did with her Special Baked Corn. My grandmother lived to be 92, but her warm smile and sharp tongue fill the room as I share this recipe with you directly from her hand written notes. Enjoy!

Fudge

1	(13 ounce) can Pet evaporated milk	1	(10½ ounce) package small marshmallows
4½	cups granulated sugar	1	teaspoon vanilla
1½	sticks margarine	1	cup nuts, chopped
3	(6 ounce) packages chocolate chips		

In a saucepan, mix together milk, sugar and margarine. Cover and bring to boil. Boil 8 minutes. Stir in chocolate chips, marshmallows, vanilla and nuts. Pour into greased pans. Let sit 12 hours before cutting.

William L. Gibbons
District Attorney General

Sweet Potato Custard

2	cups cooked mashed sweet potatoes	1	teaspoon cinnamon
¾	cup brown sugar	1	teaspoon nutmeg
4	eggs, beaten	1	teaspoon allspice
1	stick butter or margarine, melted	1	teaspoon ginger
½	cup maple syrup	1	tablespoon vanilla or almond extract
½	cup condensed milk	¼	cup rum, optional

Combine all ingredients. Pour into greased baking dish. Bake at 350 degrees until mixture is firm. If desired, you may use custard as a filler for sweet potato pie. Just pour into baked pie shell and top with marshmallows. Return to oven to lightly toast topping.

Note: Custard should pour into baking dish easily, not stiff. Taste custard for your degree of sweetness and spice before baking. You may add rum (¼ cup).

Joyce Cobb, Singer

Roasted Vegetables

	New potatoes		String beans
2	teaspoons baking soda		Baby carrots
	Virgin olive oil		Broccoli
	Lawry's garlic salt		Yellow squash
	Asparagus	¼	cup water

Boil new potatoes in water with baking soda to remove sap. Boil until water turns green. Rinse thoroughly until water is clear. Quarter potatoes and toss in olive oil and garlic salt. Wash remaining vegetables thoroughly and steam for 6 minutes, or to your discretion. Season vegetables in virgin olive oil and garlic salt. Place vegetables and new potatoes on a cookie sheet. Add ¼ cup of water. Cover with foil and cook at 300 degrees for 25 minutes.

Note: This recipe works with any vegetables. These are my favorites.

The Reverend Dr. and Mrs. Fred Lofton, Senior Pastor
Metropolitan Baptist Church

Chocolate Ice Cream

4	eggs	7	cups milk
1½	cups granulated sugar	3	cups whipping cream
2	boxes chocolate instant	2½	tablespoons vanilla
	pudding (powdered)	½	teaspoon salt

Beat eggs until light. Add sugar gradually, beating until thick. Add 2 cups milk and pudding powder. Beat until smooth. Add remaining ingredients. Mix well. Freeze in 5-quart ice cream freezer.

Yield: 1 gallon

Dave Brown
WMC-TV Channel 5

As to words of wisdom, I often think of what my Mother has said many times, "It could always be worse." I know that to be true. Sometimes it is very difficult, but I always try to find something positive in the situation. The positive outlook instilled by my mom has led me to become active in the fight against drunk drivers. After a personal tragedy, I decided that there was little or nothing good about what had happened, so it was up to me to try to see if we could make something good happen from it. I don't know if I am succeeding, but the effort seems worthy.

Banana Pound Cake

½	cup mashed bananas	½	cup sour cream
2	eggs	⅛	teaspoon cinnamon
2	tablespoons dark rum	⅛	teaspoon grated nutmeg
2	tablespoons light rum	4	tablespoons sliced
1	(17 ounce) package of		almonds
	pound cake mix		

Preheat oven to 325 degrees. Blend first 4 ingredients into pound cake mix. Mix until smooth and creamy. Beat in sour cream, cinnamon and nutmeg. Generously grease 9 x 5 x 3 inch loaf pan. Sprinkle bottom of pan with sliced almonds. Pour batter in pan. Bake for 70 to 75 minutes or until done. Leave in pan and place on wire rack to cool for 10 minutes before turning out. Cake must be completely cool before cutting.

Note: When I make it at home, I add a little more rum than called for.

Yield: 1 loaf

Earl Randall, Singer, Musician

I fell in love with this cake, got the recipe and things have been better at home since! I have been married for 29 years and I hope to go another 29 years!

Green Enchiladas

2 cans cream of
   mushroom soup
2 cans chopped green
   chiles
¼ cup chopped onions

Salt and pepper to taste
18 corn tortillas
Shredded Cheddar
   cheese

Mix soup, chiles and onions. Add salt and pepper. I use Accent too.

Spread a little in the bottom of 13 x 9 inch pan, for a thin layer of moisture on bottom. Layer 6 tortillas in bottom of pan. Top with generous portion of soup mixture, then ⅓ of cheese. Repeat layers for a total of 3 layers. Bake at 350 degrees for 30 to 45 minutes. Let sit 10 minutes before serving. This is great with frijoles, corn, salad or fruit.

Marybeth Conley
WREG-TV Channel 3

This is a favorite from my childhood, cheap and tasty! My kids even love it, and it's easy enough that my 11 year old makes it too.

Mississippi Delta Apricot Casserole

1   (#2) can apricots, peeled
½   pound light brown sugar
3   tablespoons lemon juice
½   box Cheese Ritz crackers
½   stick butter

Remove seed from apricots and drain for 1 to 1½ hours. Turn apricot cavities up in casserole dish and sprinkle with sugar and lemon juice. Marinate overnight in refrigerator. Just before cooking, crumble crackers, coarsely, over apricots. Drizzle with butter. Bake at 350 degrees for 40 to 45 minutes.

Yield: 8 servings

Nelly Galloway Shearer, State Regent,
Tennessee Daughters of the American Revolution

This recipe was given to me by my sister-in-law, Margaret Davidson. She used this for holiday and special event entertaining. It was delicious and could be served as a dessert.

Victoria Murphy's Rum Cake

CAKE

¾ cup chopped pecans, optional
1 package yellow cake mix
1 (6 ounce) package vanilla instant pudding mix, dry

½ cup oil
½ cup water
½ cup dark rum
4 eggs
   Cherries, optional

GLAZE

1 cup granulated sugar
¼ cup water

1 stick butter
¼ cup rum

Set aside pecans. Mix remaining ingredients with a blender until well blended. Spread pecans in bottom of greased Bundt pan. Pour in mixture. Bake at 350 degrees for 50 minutes or until tester comes out clean. Remove from oven and cool in pan. For glaze, bring sugar, water and butter to a boil for 7 minutes, stirring constantly. Remove from heat and add rum. Once cake is cool, remove from pan. Poke holes in cake with a big fork and brush on glaze. Continue to glaze all over the cake until glaze is gone.

Tommie Cervetti, Class of 1994, Manager
Shelby County Mayor's Office on Aging

A very special person at my church, Miss Victoria Murphy, shared this rum cake recipe with me. Miss Murphy, her two sisters and three brothers originate from Blissville, Arkansas. They later moved to Pine Bluff. Ruth Murphy, Victoria's sister, once remarked that when the Murphys left Blissville, they took the bliss with them. So, they had to change the name of the town. They later moved to Helena, residing in what is now a bed and breakfast called "The Edwardian". The Murphys finally moved to Memphis, and I had the good fortune to become friends with the sisters at St. Peter Church. Victoria rarely cooked, but she did make a mean rum cake.

Appetizers

*I was thinking I was getting to the
end of my life, but I was wrong.*

A short story about how I got interested in cooking.
10% inspiration. 90% perspiration.

Two women in my life played a great role in my productivity for culinary art. One lady, my mother, inspired me into this realm and the other woman "perspired" me to strive for perfection in it.

As a child I was a very fussy eater. I was about 9 or 10 years old when my mother calmly said, "Son if you don't like our cooking, maybe you should learn to cook of your liking." That was a turning point in my life. I started experimenting and cooking while my folks were out of the house.

My preoccupation with my gluttony served me well in my student days when I was in dormitories. As chairman of the "mess" committee, I figuratively revolutionized the menu and service. I introduced buffet serving in a hostel where for many years it was the tradition to stand in queue (line) to get served. This was in India.

In the USA where I stayed in a hostel to imbibe American culture and cuisine, I was much in demand during the weekends. My other Indian friends who opted to live in apartments were vying for my visit so that I could cook Indian food for them to please their palate. I had the best of both worlds, during the week American culture and cuisine and on the weekend Indian spiced and aromatic dishes.

Married life confronted me with a situation wherein circumstances and necessity for survival plunged me into spending more and more time in the kitchen, trying newer dishes and in volumes sufficient to feed as many as 200-300 people on some of our festivals. This was the phase where I perspired to approach perfection in many of my recipes.

Today, I find cooking a kind of therapy, unwinding and relaxing. I like to cook late at night, maybe after 9 or 10 p.m. My tribute is to my mother who indeed was an excellent cook. My sisters tell me that they can taste "mother's cooking" in my preparations. Thank you mom for your inspiration, which continues to serve me well today.

Asan G. Tejwani, Class of 1999

Aloo-Tikkee

5	large baking potatoes	½	teaspoon granulated garlic
½	cup frozen chopped spinach, thawed	½	teaspoon granulated onion
¾	cup bread crumbs	2	teaspoons lemon juice
6-8	fresh mint leaves, crushed	2	teaspoons oil
2	hot green peppers, more if desired	½	teaspoon ground ginger
			Salt to taste

Bake or boil potatoes and grate. Add remaining ingredients, kneading as if kneading dough. Add warm water, one tablespoon at a time, if needed to help stir ingredients. Form into 1 ½ inch round balls and flatten to a thick patty. Deep fry until golden brown. Serve warm with chutney and ketchup.

Asan Tejwani, Senior Leaders Board of Directors

Hot Chutney

2	medium onions, chopped	2	cups chopped fresh Chinese parsley (cilantro)
½	cup lemon juice		
2	cups chopped fresh mint	8	hot green peppers, more if desired
			Salt to taste

Blend chopped onions and lemon juice in the blender. Add mint and cilantro 1 cup at a time and puree. Add green peppers and salt and blend until fine. You may add more lemon juice to suit your taste. This makes a hot dip for hors d'oeuvres. It can also be used as a filling for sandwiches.

Asan Tejwani, Senior Leaders Board of Directors

"By working together we can help others to expand their horizons, to feel better about themselves, and to reach out to others to achieve an enhancement of the human spirit. Now our task is to transform that spirit into action, to help seniors to become informed, involved, and happy."

Lorraine Kaufman, Class of 1992 Senior Leaders Board of Directors

Hummus (Chickpeas Puree)

2	cans chickpeas, reserve juice	3	garlic cloves, peeled and chopped
⅓	cup lemon juice	¾	cup sesame oil
2	teaspoons salt		Salt to taste
			Olive Oil

Puree all ingredients including reserved juice, until smooth in consistency. Spread on a plate and cover with olive oil. Serve with pita bread.

Yield: 6 servings

Shoghig (Sunny) Ross
Senior Leaders Board of Directors

"We are not ashamed of being old, we are ashamed of what society has said that we are supposed to be like. We can change that. We can change that by drinking water. We can change that by walking, by physical fitness and by stop letting people warehouse us."

*Dick Gregory,
Actor, Activist, Athlete
and Comedian*

*Participant,
Senior Voices Project*

Ham and Cheese Rolls

2	packages Pepperidge Farm party rolls, 40 rolls	3	tablespoons poppy seeds
2	sticks butter	1	medium onion, chopped
3	tablespoons mustard		Ham
			Swiss cheese

Mix together butter, mustard, poppy seeds and onion. Cut bread in halves. Spread mixture over rolls with spatula. Cut ham and Swiss cheese the size of rolls. Make a sandwich. Cover with foil and bake at 350 degrees for 15 minutes.

Nancy Peace, Friend of Senior Leaders

Spanish Gazpacho

1	cup tomato, chopped	1	garlic clove, minced
½	cup celery, chopped	2	tablespoons wine
½	cup cucumber, chopped		vinegar
½	cup green pepper,	2	tablespoons oil
	chopped	1	teaspoon salt
¼	cup green onion,	½	teaspoon pepper
	chopped	½	teaspoon Worcestershire
2½	cups tomatoes		sauce

Combine first 5 ingredients and set aside. In a bowl, blend remaining ingredients. Combine all ingredients and chill at least 4 hours.

Yield: 4 cups

Note: For a smoother consistency, I chop the ingredients in the food processor all together starting with celery, cucumber, green pepper and garlic. Then add tomatoes and remaining ingredients.

Robert McFalls, Honorary Class of 1996

"I would tell them I think they should get involved because it has motivated me and got me to thinking. I really enjoyed it and I am not fixing to stop here. I think more positively. It used to be if somebody said something I would think 'well, that is not important', but now it makes me look at both sides."

LIFE Graduate

Spinach Sandwiches

1	(10 ounce) package frozen chopped spinach, thawed and squeezed dry	1	(6 ounce) can water chestnuts, minced
1	box dry vegetable soup mix	12	ounces fat-free sour cream
		¾	cup mayonnaise
			Chopped green onion to taste

Mix ingredients well and spread on squares of party rye.

Mal Shapiro, Class of 1994

Kelly's Homemade Pico de Gallo

2	ripe Roma tomatoes	1	can green chiles, chopped
2	ripe regular or other tomatoes	½	tablespoon olive oil
	Fresh cilantro to taste		Garlic to taste
1	chopped onion		Cumin to taste
			Fresh lime juice to taste

Finely chop tomatoes, cilantro and onion. Place in a large bowl. Add green chiles, olive oil, garlic, and cumin. Add lime juice. Chill before serving.

Kelly Duke, Friend of Senior Leaders

This is a great party dish. It is also great for Mexican dinners. This is a Kelly original. I figured salsa did not look too hard, so I tried to make it. With a little advice from an uncle who is a great cook, and a couple of looks through some cookbooks, I was ready to try my own version. You can add anything you want to the recipe such as corn or olives.

Spinach Dip

1	(10 ounce) package frozen chopped spinach	1	cup mayonnaise
1	package soup mix	1	(8 ounce) can water chestnuts, drained and chopped
1½	cups sour cream	3	green onions, chopped

Thaw and squeeze frozen spinach until almost dry. Mix all ingredients together. Blend well. Cover and chill for 2 hours. Stir before serving.

Note: This is very good served in a loaf of Hawaiian bread. Just carve the top of the bread and spoon in dip. Break up bread top in bite-sized pieces and arrange around dish.

Merle Smith, Class of 1998

Rye Bread Boat

1	round loaf seedless rye bread, unsliced	2	tablespoons chopped dry onions
2	cups sour cream	2	tablespoons parsley
2	cups mayonnaise	5	ounces dried beef
2	teaspoons dill weed	2	teaspoons Beau Monde

Remove beef from package. Run under cold water to rinse. Shake or pat dry. Stack and cut into ¾ x 1 inch squares. In a large bowl, combine all ingredients except bread. Mix well, cover and chill for 3 to 4 hours. With a sharp knife, cut a circle in top of rye bread. Remove top. Hollow out loaf leaving ½ inch wall. Break removed bread into bite-sized pieces. Place loaf on serving platter. Pour mixture into hollowed out bread. Arrange pieces around loaf on platter. Serve immediately.

Note: Beau Monde is a special spice made from a mixture of ground celery seed, onion powder and salt. If you can't find it, you can mix equal parts of the three seasonings. My daughter mixes her own, and it works perfectly.

JoAnn Davis, Enterprise National Bank

This is a great recipe for a crowd. Those who have never seen it will, at first, hesitate to try it. But it is absolutely wonderful! Great for holiday gatherings, football Saturdays or informal get-togethers. When the bread pieces are gone, pull pieces from the main loaf.

"In 5 years, I won't be too far from 100. I hope I will still be able to go. I ride somewhere on the City bus almost every day. I hope I will be able to still do the things I do now like mowing my yard, baking and helping people."

Victoria Smith,
Class of 1994

Cheese Krispies

2	sticks butter	½	pound sharp cheese, shredded
2	cups all-purpose flour	¼	teaspoon red pepper
½	teaspoon salt	2	cups rice crisp cereal

Cream butter. Add flour, salt, cheese and red pepper. Mix well. Add rice crisp cereal and shape into small balls. Flatten on cookie sheet and bake at 350 degrees for 12 to 15 minutes.

Robert McFalls, Honorary Class of 1996

Cheese Sticks

6	tablespoons butter	1	cup milk
2¼	cups self-rising flour	1	cup extra sharp
1	tablespoon granulated		Cheddar cheese,
	sugar		grated

Melt butter in 9 x 13 inch pan. Mix all other ingredients. Kneed 10 times on floured surface. Pat into a flat oblong shape. Cut strips length wise. Roll each strip in melted butter and arrange in pan. Bake at 325 degrees for 15 to 20 minutes.

Libby Bilderbeck, Friend of Senior Leaders

Guacamole Dip

4	ripe avocados	1	fresh lime, juiced
½	medium white onion,	½	teaspoon salt
	finely chopped or	½	teaspoon cayenne
	grated		pepper
1	teaspoon garlic powder	½	teaspoon salsa jalapeño
1	fresh lemon, juiced		

Mash avocados. Whip all ingredients together and refrigerate until serving time. Serve with tortilla chips and a pitcher of margaritas.

Nelda Grimes, Class of 1992

This recipe was given to me by my dear friend Pat West with whom I exchanged many wonderful recipes.

Mexican Tuna Dip

1   (7 ounce) can solid
    white tuna packed in
    water
½   onion, grated
¾   cup mayonnaise

2   tablespoons lemon juice
4   teaspoons hot jalapeño
    salsa
    Crushed red pepper to
    taste

Drain tuna and mash with a fork. Set aside. In a medium mixing bowl, combine onion, mayonnaise, lemon juice and salsa. Mix until well combined. Stir in tuna, blending well. Transfer to a serving bowl, cover and chill for 1 hour. Sprinkle with red pepper before serving.

Note: It is delicious with corn chips and fresh vegetables such as broccoli, zucchini, mushrooms and cauliflower.

Yield: 1½ cups

Sallye Thomas, Class of 1997

This easy, but lively, tuna dip is a great way to lift the spirits. It makes a flavorful beginning for any meal even if you don't have a south-of-the-border menu.

Fresh Fruit Dip

1   cup marshmallow cream
1   cup mayonnaise
1   tablespoon grated
    orange rind

1   teaspoon cinnamon
½   teaspoon ground
    nutmeg
2   teaspoons honey

Mix together all ingredients thoroughly. Chill 3 hours or overnight. Serve with assorted fresh fruit.

Jennie Morring, Class of 1993

Shrimp Dip

1	(3½ ounce) can shrimp	5	tablespoons mayonnaise-type salad dressing
1	(8 ounce) package cream cheese	½	small onion, diced
1	teaspoon Worcestershire sauce		Milk

Mix all ingredients together, and add milk until it reaches a dipping consistency.

Note: Any leftover dip is great for sandwich spread.

Beverlee Timm, Class of 1994

Pesto and Cream Cheese on Sun-Dried Tomatoes

PESTO

2	cups fresh basil leaves	¾	cup freshly grated Parmesan cheese
4	cloves garlic		Salt and pepper to taste
½	cup pine nuts		
¾	cup olive oil, more if desired		

CHEESE FILLING

1	cup sun-dried tomatoes packed in olive oil, drained and chopped	2	(8 ounce) packages cream cheese, sliced to ½ inch

Mix all Pesto ingredients in a food processor. Pulse until Pesto is at a desired consistency. Set aside. Drain and chop tomatoes. Set aside. Whip cream cheese until fluffy. Spread tomatoes onto a serving platter. Pour cream cheese over tomatoes. Chill for 2 hours. Garnish with Pesto sauce. Serve with your favorite crackers.

Terry Adams, Friend of Senior Leaders

Christmas Nuts

½ cup butter
2 egg whites, stiff-beaten
1 cup granulated sugar
    Dash of salt

1 tablespoon vanilla
½ cup slivered almonds
1 cup walnut halves
2 cups pecans

Melt butter in a 15½ x 10½ x 1 inch jelly-roll pan. Fold sugar and salt into egg whites. Beat until stiff peaks form. Add vanilla. Mix. Fold nuts into mixture. Pour into buttered pan. Bake at 325 degrees for 30 minutes turning every 10 minutes, or until nuts are browned and no butter remains in pan. Cool.

Note: Do not dry on a paper towel. Nuts will stick and not come loose. I have tried whole almonds and sliced almonds. Neither work as well as slivered. Peanuts, Spanish peanuts and cashews do not work.

Yield: 4 cups

Dorothy Conyers, Class of 2000

This is my main present I send to my family and friends during the holidays. I make about 6 to 8 times the recipe.

Fat-Free Fruit Cheese Ball

1 (8 ounce) package fat-free cream cheese
2 (3 ounce) packages sugar-free vanilla pudding mix

1 (3 ounce) can crushed pineapple, drained
1 (20 ounce) can fruit cocktail, drained

Mix together cream cheese and pudding mix. Add crushed pineapple and fruit cocktail. Mix well. Form into a ball. Chill for 2 hours. Serve with fat-free crackers.

Helen Lockhart, Class of 1995

When I went to LIFE class, I was experiencing deep grief at the loss of my husband. My whole life had been focused on him. In LIFE class, I realized that there were many opportunities to help make things better in the community. I also made new friends. I am active, healthy, and giving something back to the community. I know my husband would be proud of me and I feel great!

LIFE Graduate

Sweet Potato Cheese Ball

1	(8 ounce) package cream cheese, softened	2	cups shredded sharp Cheddar cheese
½	cup cooked mashed sweet potatoes	¼	cup crushed pineapple, well drained
1	(2½ ounce) package smoked beef, chopped	1	tablespoon chopped onion

Combine cream cheese and potatoes. Mix well. Stir in beef, cheese, pineapple and onion. Form into a ball and chill. Serve with crackers.

Johnnie Harrison, Class of 1997

Artichoke Squares

2	(6 ounce) jars marinated artichokes		Dash Tabasco sauce
1	onion, chopped	½	teaspoon oregano
1	garlic clove, minced		Salt and pepper to taste
4	eggs	2	cups shredded Cheddar cheese
¼	cup bread crumbs		

Drain juice from 1 jar of artichokes. Pour into skillet. Sauté onion and garlic in oil and juice. Drain other jar and discard juice. Chop both jars of artichokes. In separate bowl, beat eggs. Add bread crumbs and spices. Stir in onion mixture, cheese and artichokes. Mix well. Pour into greased 9 x 13 inch pan. Bake at 325 degrees for 30 minutes. Cut into squares and serve hot.

Yield: 30 squares

Robert McFalls, Honorary Class of 1996

Cocktail Meatballs

1 pound ground beef	Salt and pepper to taste
½ cup Italian bread crumbs	1 (16 ounce) jar chili sauce
1 onion, finely chopped	1 (6 ounce) jar grape jelly
1 egg, slightly beaten	

Mix ground beef, bread crumbs, onion, egg, salt and pepper. Shape into walnut sized meatballs. Place on cookie sheet and bake at 350 degrees for 30 minutes. Mix chili sauce and grape jelly and boil in a heavy skillet for 5 minutes. Place meatballs in a serving dish and cover with chili sauce mixture. Serve warm.

Eileen Stephenson, Class of 1993

In LIFE class, I learned not to define myself as an old person, or a diabetic, or needy person. I learned to define myself as who I know myself to be. I'm a free spirit. I'm losing my cocoon of all those labels.

Cheese Roll

1 (2 ounce) wedge Roquefort cheese	¼ cup pimento, chopped
1 pound hoop cheese, grated	½ cup chopped sweet pickle
1 (4 ounce) package blue cheese, softened	1 teaspoon savory salt, optional
1 (8 ounce) package cream cheese, softened	1½ cups chopped pecans, optional
½ teaspoon garlic powder or onion powder	Chili powder

Mash and mix all ingredients thoroughly. Shape into 4 rolls. Roll in chili powder until covered. Chill before serving.

Jennie Morring, Class of 1993

This recipe was given to me by D. Embry. She was a good friend, and we worked together for many years. We first met at the old Mallory Air Force Depot. She was an excellent cook, and her cheese rolls graced many a party.

Olive Cheese Balls

15	ounces sharp cheese, grated	½	cup plus 2 tablespoons all-purpose flour
3	tablespoons butter	¼	teaspoon pepper
½	teaspoon salt	85	green olives

Cream cheese and butter. Add salt, flour and pepper. Shape into 1 inch balls using olives for center. Freeze for at least 24 hours. Bake at 400 degrees for 10 minutes when frozen. Serve at room temperature.

Linda Nichols, Honorary Class of 1996

For the past 10 years, we have had a Christmas party where a group of friends rent a small trolley bus and drive around looking at Christmas lights. We all bring "trolley food" which has to go with champagne and be easy to eat with your fingers. This recipe is what everyone requests from me.

The world is not what it use to be. That's for sure. But we continue to change no matter how old we get. You don't have to teach an old dog new tricks. We can learn them on our own.

Bourbon Bites

| 3 | pounds wieners | 1 | cup brown sugar |
| 1 | cup tomato sauce or ketchup | 1 | cup bourbon whiskey |

Cut wieners into bite-size pieces and place in a large pot. Combine tomato sauce, brown sugar and bourbon. Pour sauce mixture over wieners leaving room in the pot for expansion. Cover and cook at 350 degrees for 3 hours. These are extra tasty if cooked the day before and reheated.

Jennie Morring, Class of 1993

Olive-Cream Cheese Spread

2 (8 ounce) packages cream cheese, softened	3 tablespoons creamy horseradish sauce
1 cup pimento stuffed olives, cut	½ cup ranch type dressing

Mix all ingredients thoroughly. Use as a sandwich spread or serve on crackers.

Yield: 3 cups

Committee

"I'm legally deaf and blind. I have no patience with people who just sit down and give up. If you don't see well, find out how you can improve it... I think attitude is the most important ingredient of life. We can mope and stew, people won't like you, they'll stay away from you. If you approach things like, 'I can do it. If someone else did it, I can try.' I've found that people are just much more friendly."

Novella Schulte, Class of 1995

Cheese and Sausage Balls

1 pound sausage	1 pound sharp Cheddar cheese, grated
4 cups biscuit mix	Tabasco sauce to taste

Mix sausage and biscuit mix. Add cheese and Tabasco sauce. Mix well. Form into small balls, about ½ inch in diameter. Bake at 350 degrees for 20 minutes or until golden brown.

L. Almarita Johnson, Class of 1993

Bloody Mary Dip

1 cup sour cream
½ cup plain yogurt
½ cup mayonnaise or
  salad dressing
1 envelope Bloody Mary
  cocktail mix

⅛ teaspoon salt
2 tablespoons sliced green
  onions
  Celery stick dippers

In a small bowl, combine sour cream, yogurt, mayonnaise, dry cocktail mix and salt. Stir in green onions. Cover and chill 3 hours or overnight. Sprinkle with additional green onion slices if desired. Serve with celery stick dippers.

Jennie Morring, Class of 1993

Our generation has been blessed. We owe it to our grandchildren to give something back.

LIFE Class Participant, 1992

The True MAN's Recipes

Baked Beans

1 can Bush's Original Baked Beans

Open can, pour into dish. Put into microwave until warm. Serve.

Summer Time Cool Treat Coke Float

2 big dips of vanilla ice cream

Coca-Cola

Put ice cream in a tall soda glass. Finish filling with coca cola.
Serve under a big shade tree in the back yard with a straw and soda spoon.

Bone Tired Hungry Dinner

Come home and fall on sofa.
Tell wife what to cook for dinner.
Wife tells you, "We are eating out."

Easy Breakfast

Go walk two miles at the mall. Stop at K-Mart on your way home.
Buy 3 donuts. Go home. Serve with coffee.

Chris Glass, Class of 1996

Cleo's Country Fried Steak

1	medium round steak, cut into serving pieces	½	bell pepper, chopped
	Salt and pepper to taste	1	(10 ounce) can golden mushroom soup
	Flour for coating steak	½	soup can water
1	small onion, chopped		

Season round steak with salt and pepper. Coat with flour. Place in a skillet with hot oil and brown on both sides. In a separate skillet, sauté onion and bell pepper. Pour off excess oils. Put round steak in with onion and bell pepper. Combine soup and water and pour over top of steak. Cover and cook over low heat for 30 minutes.

Vanessa Grant, Friend of Senior Leaders

I cherish the memory of my Dad on Sundays cooking for his family. He would cook the most tender and delicious steak smothered in onions and gravy. If you are like me, struggling to master the secret of how to cook steak, you will be pleasantly surprised. Just try this recipe. It is so tender that when you place the first bite in your mouth the other bites will be just as tender as the first.

When I came to LIFE class, I was reluctant to even talk about getting older. I felt like the world had stereotyped older people as somehow "less than." But I was leaving class one day and I realized I felt proud of being 75. I felt proud of me.

Colorful Kabobs

1 pound top sirloin	1 red pepper
3-4 boneless, skinless	1 yellow pepper
chicken breasts	Italian dressing
Worcestershire sauce to	Cavendar's Greek
taste	seasoning to taste
Onion salt to taste	Ground mustard to taste
Garlic salt to taste	Pesto, optional
1 large purple onion	2 cups white rice
1 green bell pepper	

Season beef and chicken with spices to taste. Place on grill for 10 minutes until meat begins to change color. Cut onion and peppers into ½ dollar sized chunks. Pull meat from grill and cut into similar sized pieces. Using skewers, arrange vegetables and meats alternating so that a tasty and tasteful combination appears. Be consistent in the arrangement. Laying all skewers on a cookie sheet, dose liberally with Italian dressing. Dust with Cavendar's Greek seasoning, ground mustard and pesto. Place skewers on grill for approximately 10 to 15 minutes or until done. Serve over a bed of rice.

Ken Hall, Friend of Senior Leaders

I like to make kabobs for dinner parties because they look good and have "something for everybody." I particularly enjoyed serving these to my parents last year on Mother's Day. It was a flashback to the far distant past when I squirmed at many a meal trying to hide my English peas and other less than favorite vegetables. The memory returned vividly when I watched with amusement my father quietly push around on his plate the various peppers he didn't like.

6 in 1 Casserole

1	pound ground beef	2	(13 ounce) cans carrots
4	medium potatoes, quartered	1	(10¾ ounce) can tomato soup
2	medium onions, sliced		Salt and pepper to taste
2	(13 ounce) cans English peas		

Drain peas and carrots reserving liquid. Mix reserved liquid with soup. Set aside. Brown ground beef and place in greased casserole dish. Layer potatoes, onions, peas and carrots over beef. Pour soup mixture over top. Sprinkle with salt and pepper. Cover and cook at 350 degrees for 1 hour or until vegetables are done.

Jackie Hill, Class of 1992

Aging is not about "them, the elderly." It is about us. We are all aging. That's the beauty of it.

This dish was made by my aunt, with whom I lived, during World War II when food was rationed. I was just a child, but as I remember and have since heard, each member of a household received a certain number of food ration stamps each month. Some items were very scarce and people would save stamps for special foods for special occasions.

Enchilada Casserole

1	pound ground beef	¼	pound shredded Cheddar cheese
1	(4 ounce) can green chiles, chopped	1	(10 ounce) can cream of mushroom soup
1	small onion, chopped	12	tortillas
	Garlic powder to taste		
1	(10 ounce) can enchilada sauce		

In a skillet, combine ground beef, chiles, onion and garlic powder. Brown over medium heat and simmer. Dip tortillas in enchilada sauce and place in a casserole dish. Layer over tortillas alternating with meat mixture, cheese and soup. Pour remaining enchilada sauce over top. Bake at 450 degrees for 20 minutes.

Beverlee Timm, Class of 1994

I laughed and cried in LIFE class. Who said seniors don't have a sense of humor? Did I mention that I also found out I liked to paint. Who knows, maybe I'll be the next Grandma Moses?

Quick Winter Day Warmup

1	medium onion, diced		Salt and pepper to taste
1	medium bell pepper, diced	1	(15 ounce) can kidney beans
2	celery stalks, diced	¾	cup tomato paste
2	cups water	1	teaspoon granulated sugar
1½	pounds ground chuck		
1	tablespoon chili powder		

In a large saucepan, cook onion, bell pepper and celery in water on low heat. Brown ground chuck in skillet. Drain fat and add meat to onion mixture. Stir. Add chili powder, salt and pepper. Rinse kidney beans in colander until clear of liquid. Add beans and tomato paste to meat mixture. Cover and cook on low heat 30 minutes, stirring occasionally. Add sugar and cook an additional 10 to 15 minutes on medium heat. Serve with saltines, cheese toast or grilled cheese sandwich.

Doris Quinn, Class of 1995

My children seemed to especially enjoy this as a Saturday meal on cold days when they would be outside raking leaves, roller skating or bike riding. It was a real treat for them. I can still remember them coming in from the fall or winter chill and playing games. It was also a great quick, hot meal to prepare after working all day at the Regional Medical Center. I still cook this Winter Day Warmup dish occasionally for my grown kids when they visit. Even my grandchildren really enjoy it.

"Crock" Steak

1	onion, chopped	1	round steak, tenderized
½	pint mushrooms, cut		and cut into serving
	into pieces		pieces
1½	cups all-purpose flour	1	cup beef bouillon
	Seasoning to taste	⅔	cup red wine

In a skillet, brown onion and mushroom in oil until tender. Remove and set aside. In a large bowl, sift together flour and seasoning. Coat steak pieces in seasoned flour and lay in skillet with oil. Brown both sides. Add bouillon, ⅓ cup wine, onions and mushrooms. Cover and simmer for 1½ hours, stirring occasionally. Add remaining wine just prior to serving. Great with rice and vegetables.

Shirley Minor, Class of 1992

In LIFE class, I learned to love me. I learned that this is the first step to empowerment. I am worthy no matter what my age.

Marinated Bourbon Steak

½	cup bourbon	½	teaspoon cracked black
2	tablespoons lemon juice		pepper
2	teaspoons brown sugar	2	(1 inch) top loin strip
			steaks

Combine first four ingredients in a shallow dish. Add steaks and turn to coat. Cover and refrigerate 4 hours, turning occasionally. Remove steaks and discard marinade. Cook, covered, for 8 minutes on each side.

Evelyn Cornelius, Class of 1993

Chili Con Carne

3	tablespoons oil or bacon fat	1	(16 ounce) can red kidney beans
1	onion, sliced	2	cups stewed canned tomatoes or tomato sauce
1	clove garlic		
1	pound ground beef	1	tablespoon chili powder

In a large skillet, heat oil and sauté onion for 2 minutes. Put garlic on a toothpick and add to onion. Cook 5 minutes, stirring regularly. Add ground beef, beans, tomatoes and chili powder. Simmer 1 hour. Add salt and pepper. Remove garlic clove. Serve.

Yield: 6 servings

Pearl Hollins, Class of 1995

This is one of the recipes I used to use on Saturdays during the winter months when my children were growing up. They liked it very much. I would serve it with candied yams, potatoes and Kool Aid.

Southwestern-Style Meatloaf

2	pounds ground beef	1	cup soft bread crumbs
1	teaspoon chili powder	1	medium onion, chopped
¾	teaspoon salt	⅓	cup chopped green peppers
⅛	teaspoon pepper		Green pepper strips, optional
⅓	cup barbecue sauce		
2	eggs, beaten		
1	(8¼ ounce) whole kernel corn, drained and chopped		

Place ground beef in large mixing bowl. Sprinkle chili powder, salt and pepper over beef. Add barbecue sauce, eggs, corn, bread crumbs, onion and green pepper. Mix lightly, but thoroughly. Shape beef mixture into 10 (4 inch) loafs. Place on rack in open roasting pan. Bake at 350 degrees for 1½ hours. Garnish with green pepper strips.

Sandra Engelhardt, Friend of Senior Leaders

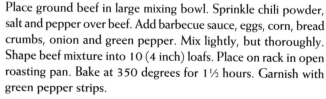

Meatloaf I

1½ pounds ground beef
1 cup crushed crackers
1 (4 ounce) can
  mushroom stems and
  pieces, drained
1 egg
2 cloves garlic, minced
¼ cup minced onion
¼ cup evaporated milk

Mix together all ingredients thoroughly. Add more milk if needed to hold mixture together. Bake in a loaf pan at 350 degrees until done, approximately 45 minutes.

Nelda Grimes, Class of 1992

Meatloaf II

1 pound ground beef
½ cup cream of wheat
  cereal uncooked
3 tablespoons finely
  chopped onion,
  optional
¾ teaspoon salt
Dash ground black
  pepper
2 tablespoons ketchup
2 tablespoons water
1 egg
Ketchup

Preheat oven to 350 degrees. In a mixing bowl, combine first five ingredients. In a separate bowl, combine ketchup, water and egg. Mix into meat mixture with fork until combined. Form into loaf. Place in shallow baking pan. Cook for 50 minutes or until done. Brush loaf with ketchup during last 15 minutes of cooking.

Yield: 5 servings

Louise Fowler, Friend of Senior Leaders

I think its odd how people talk about us seniors and our love life. I hear younger people saying, "Isn't that cute. They are holding hands." We're not cute. Cute is for puppies. We are adults who love even more deeply than we did when we were younger. Holding hands still has that magic!

Beef Oriental

2	onions, chopped	1	(10 ounce) can
1	cup celery, chopped		mushroom soup
3	tablespoons butter	1½	cups water chestnuts,
½	cup uncooked rice		sliced
1	pound ground beef	½	cup soy sauce
1	(10 ounce) can chicken	¼	teaspoon pepper
	soup	1	pound can bean sprouts
		3	cups Chinese noodles

Brown onion and celery in butter. Add rice and beef and brown. Combine next five ingredients in 2-quart casserole dish. Add beef mixture. Gently stir in bean sprouts. Bake covered at 325 degrees for 30 minutes. Uncover and bake 20 minutes. Serve over noodles.

L. Almarita Johnson, Class of 1993

Italian Spaghetti

2	pounds round steak, diced	1	teaspoon thyme
		2	carrots, chopped
2	tablespoons olive oil	3	cloves garlic, chopped
2	medium onions, chopped	1	pound spaghetti noodles, cooked and drained
1	(14 ounce) can tomatoes		Salt and pepper to taste
½	cup parsley, lightly packed		Parmesan cheese, optional

Brown steak in olive oil until golden. Add onions and brown. In a saucepan, heat tomatoes, parsley, thyme, carrots and garlic. Let simmer. Add meat and onions to tomato mixture. Add salt and pepper to taste. Simmer 2 to 3 hours, stirring often until thickened. Serve over noodles. Top with cheese.

L. Almarita Johnson, Class of 1993

Lila's Spaghetti

3	ounces spaghetti noodles, cooked	1	(20 ounce) jar chunky spaghetti sauce
1½	pound ground chuck	1	teaspoon oregano
3	tablespoons chopped onion	1	teaspoon Italian seasoning
3	tablespoons chopped bell pepper		

Brown ground chuck, onion and bell pepper. Drain. Add spaghetti sauce and remaining ingredients. Add small amount of water if sauce becomes too thick. Combine sauce and cooked spaghetti.

Lila Black, Friend of Senior Leaders

"Our age does not define who we are."

Three Bean Chili

1	teaspoon olive oil	1	medium turnip, cubed
1	medium onion, chopped	2	stalks celery, coarsely chopped
1	(16 ounce) can black beans	2	cups vegetable stock
2	cups cooked lima beans	1½	cups tomato juice
1	(15 ounce) can soybeans, not rinsed or 2 cups mature soybeans	3½	ounces diced green chiles
		1	teaspoon red chili powder
		1	teaspoon cumin powder

In a large pot, heat olive oil over medium-high heat. Add onion and cook 15 minutes until onion is deep golden. Add remaining ingredients. Stir gently. Bring to boil. Reduce heat and simmer 10 to 15 minutes until vegetables are soft.

Yield: 6 servings

Bill Ramsey, Friend of Senior Leaders

I wish I had been able to take a LIFE class 20 or even 40 years ago. What I learned in class really applies to people of all ages. I have to know what I want and go after it. I don't have to wait for others to say it's okay.

Turkey Stuffing

2	pounds ground round	¼	cup raisins
4	stalks celery, chopped	1	(1 pint) jar fresh oysters
1	large onion, chopped		

In a large skillet, combine ground round, celery and onion. Cover and simmer until beef is cooked. Drain grease. Mix in raisins and oysters. Stuff turkey with stuffing in last ½ hour of baking.

Theresa Hudson, Class of 1992

This recipe is long standing in my family and is prepared only on Thanksgiving. What makes this recipe special is the fresh oysters.

Shepherd's Pie

1	pound ground beef	1	stick butter
1	small onion, chopped	½	cup milk
2	cups beef gravy		Salt and pepper to taste
4	medium potatoes		

Brown beef with onion. Add gravy. Boil and mash potatoes with butter, milk, salt and pepper. Place ground beef mixture into casserole dish. Top with potatoes. Bake at 350 degrees for 25 minutes or until bubbly.

Beverlee Timm, Class of 1994

This is an updated version of an old Scottish recipe. When I lived in Scotland I learned to make this. It has always been a favorite of my children. My grown son still says when I make this he wants it all for himself.

Savory Vegetarian Shepherd's Pie

Great vegetarian version of a hearty classic.

3	small potatoes	1	(10 ounce) package
2	cloves garlic, minced		frozen whole kernel
½	teaspoon dried basil,		corn or mixed
	crushed		vegetables
2	tablespoons margarine	1	(8 ounce) can tomato
¼	teaspoon salt		sauce
2-4	tablespoons milk	1	teaspoon Worcestershire
1	medium onion, chopped		sauce
1	medium carrot, sliced	½	teaspoon granulated
1	tablespoon oil		sugar
1	(15 ounce) can kidney	1	cup shredded Cheddar
	beans, rinsed and		cheese
	drained		Paprika, optional
1	(14½ ounce) can whole		
	tomatoes		

Peel and quarter potatoes. Boil, covered, in a small amount of lightly salted water for 20 to 25 minutes or until tender. Drain. Mash potatoes. In a small saucepan, cook garlic and basil in margarine for 15 seconds. Add to potatoes along with salt. Gradually beat in enough milk to make light and fluffy. Set aside. For filling, in a medium saucepan cook onion and carrot in hot oil until onion is tender but not brown. Stir in beans, tomatoes, frozen vegetables, tomato sauce, Worcestershire sauce and sugar. Heat until bubbly. Transfer vegetable mixture to 8 x 8 x 2 inch baking dish. Drop mashed potatoes in 4 mounds over vegetable mixture. Sprinkle with Cheddar cheese and paprika. Bake, uncovered, at 375 degrees for 25 to 30 minutes or until cheese begins to brown.

Yield: 4 servings

Bill Baker, Senior Leaders Age Stage Director

"I've always been interested in learning new things. I get bored, and something new is right up my alley. So I went through the LIFE Class, I learned more and more. I made such wonderful friends. It's been wonderful, and aging has really become a whole new experience with a whole new set of people."

Jennie Morring,
Class of 1993

Murgha-E-Mohabat

Deluxe Chicken Curry

The best memory for me is the one I make tomorrow.

4	chicken legs or breasts		Pinch ground cinnamon
2½	teaspoons salt		Pinch ground cloves
½	teaspoon pepper	1	inch fresh ginger root, finely chopped
1	teaspoon garlic powder		
2	large onions, diced	1	teaspoon coriander powder
3	tablespoons oil		
8	ounces sour cream	1	teaspoon chili powder
3	ounces tomato paste	1	teaspoon turmeric
1	green chili pepper, cut fine (optional)	1	whole cardamom, crushed
2	bay leaves, crushed	1	teaspoon cumin

Lightly sprinkle salt, pepper and garlic powder on chicken. Bake at 375 degrees for 1 to 1½ hours or until done. Remove skins. Cook onions in oil until light brown. Add sour cream, tomato paste and remaining ingredients. Bring to simmer. Add chicken, turning to coat each piece. Simmer 15 minutes on low heat. If mixture gets too thick add water to desired consistency. Can be refrigerated up to 8 hours. Heat before serving.

Asan G. Tejwani, Senior Leaders Board of Directors

Pork Chops "Cola"

8	pork chops ¾ inch thick	½	cup ketchup
16	ounces cola		Salt to taste

Mix ketchup with cola. Salt pork chops and place in baking dish. Bake covered at 300 degrees for 2 hours.

Yield: 6 to 8 servings

Committee

French-Fried Onion Chicken

6	chicken breast halves, boneless	½	teaspoon salt
¾	cup grated Parmesan cheese	½	cup dry bread crumbs
		¼	teaspoon pepper
1	(3 ounce) can French-fried onions, crushed	1	egg, beaten
		2	tablespoons milk
½	teaspoon paprika	¾	cup butter, melted

Combine cheese, crushed onions, paprika, salt, bread crumbs and pepper. Set aside. In a medium bowl, mix together egg and milk. Dip chicken in egg mixture then coat in cheese mixture. Place in greased baking dish. Drizzle butter over coated chicken. Cover and bake at 350 degrees for 45 minutes. Uncover and bake for 15 minutes or until golden brown.

Yield: 6 servings

Mary Jo Williams, Friend of Senior Leaders

"Some people think that seniors are in the way. If they stop to listen and then follow in our footprints they will most likely succeed in life. No, we are not in the way, we are here to make a difference."

Helen D. Scott
LIFE Graduate,
Class of 1999
Philadelphia, PA

Vegetarian Boston Roast

4	cups cooked black-eyed peas or kidney beans	Paprika or red pepper to taste
2	cups grated cheese	Bread crumbs

Mash peas. Add cheese and Paprika. Mix in bread crumbs until mixture is stiff enough to form into a roll. Bake at 350 degrees for 45 minutes.

L. Almarita Johnson, Class of 1993

This was a good alternative to just warming up those leftover peas or beans. When I first served this, I received compliments for making "something out of nothing."

Edie's Barbecue Chicken

1	whole chicken	1	tablespoon lemon juice
3	tablespoons catsup	3	tablespoons brown
2	tablespoons vinegar		sugar
2	tablespoons Lea &	1	teaspoon paprika
	Perrins	1	teaspoon salt
4	tablespoons water	1	teaspoon chili pepper
2	tablespoons butter		

Cut chicken into desired parts. In a large saucepan, heat next 8 ingredients until butter melts. Arrange chicken in a baking dish. Sprinkle salt and pepper over pieces. Pour sauce over each piece. Bake at 450 degrees for 10 minutes. Reduce heat to 350 degrees and bake for 1 hour or until tender. Serve with white rice using sauce as gravy.

Tommie Cervetti, Class of 1994

Edith Bowers, the Grandmother of my sons, gave me this recipe in 1969. It has always been one of their favorites.

Unique Chicken Breasts

4	boneless chicken	1	cup fresh raspberries
	breasts	½	cup red table wine
	Flour to dust	½	cup chicken stock
1	tablespoon oil	½	teaspoon salt
1	bunch shallots or green	¼	teaspoon pepper
	onion, chopped		Garnish of choice

Dust chicken in flour and brown in skillet with oil. Add shallots or green onions, raspberries, wine, chicken stock, salt and pepper. Cook until chicken is thoroughly cooked. Remove chicken and cook remaining sauce until thick. Pour sauce over chicken. Add garnish and serve.

Jack Range, Friend of Senior Leaders

Apple Stuffed Chicken Breasts

6	skinless chicken breasts	¼	cup chopped pecans or walnuts
1½	cups finely diced red or green apples	3	tablespoons minced onion
¼	cup golden seedless raisins	⅔	teaspoon rubbed sage

APPLE GLAZE

¼	cup orange juice concentrate	¼	cup butter
⅓	cup apple jelly	¼	cup dry sherry

Preheat oven to 350 degrees. Place chicken breasts between sheets of waxed paper and pound with rolling pin or meat mallet until ¼ inch thick. Combine apples, raisins, nuts, onion and sage. Place a spoonful of mixture on each chicken breast. Roll up each chicken breast tucking in all sides. Secure with toothpick and place in a baking dish. In a saucepan, combine all apple glaze ingredients and simmer 2 to 3 minutes. Bake chicken breasts uncovered for 45 minutes, brushing frequently with apple glaze.

Pearl Hollins, Class of 1995

Chicken Divan

2	(10 ounce) packages frozen, chopped broccoli	1	cup mayonnaise
3-4	cups cooked, diced chicken	¼	cup milk
		1	teaspoon curry powder
2	(10¾ ounce) cans cream of chicken soup	1	cup toasted bread croutons or Chinese noodles

Cook broccoli as directed. Spread into casserole dish. Mix together chicken, soup, mayonnaise, milk and curry powder. Pour over broccoli. Top with croutons. Bake at 350 degrees for 30 minutes.

Georgia Bartosch, Class of 1992

"I was real hesitant, my spirits were low. My spirit was screaming to get out of this aging body, and be with people, and learn what's going on. And I felt real fulfilled in class. Bridget encouraged me to come, although I have hearing and sight deficits. And I've loved coming and getting to know the wonderful things that are available and to be with wonderful people. And be able to expound on what we needed to learn and find out what was available. It's been just great."

Novella Schulte, Class of 1995

Chicken Reuben

4	whole boneless chicken breasts, halved	1	cup low calorie Russian dressing
¼	teaspoon salt	4	slices low-fat Swiss cheese
½	teaspoon pepper		
2	cups sauerkraut, rinsed and drained	1	tablespoon chopped parsley, optional

Preheat oven to 325 degrees. Place chicken in nonstick baking dish. Sprinkle with salt and pepper. Cover chicken with sauerkraut. Pour dressing evenly over all and top with Swiss cheese. Cover with foil. Bake for 1 hour. Sprinkle with parsley before serving.

Anonymous

Chicken Enchiladas

1	fryer size chicken	6	(5 inch) flour or corn tortillas
1	bunch green onions, chopped	1	(10 ounce) jar enchilada sauce
½	bell pepper, chopped		Fresh cilantro
¼	cup oil		

CHEESE SAUCE
½	pound Jack cheese	1	cup milk
1	cup sour cream		

Boil chicken, debone, skin and chop. Place chicken, green onions and bell pepper in a skillet with oil and sauté. Set aside. Fry tortillas lightly, drain on paper napkins. Drop meat mixture onto tortillas. Roll, starting at end and fold down. Pour enchilada sauce into bottom of a baking pan. Place enchiladas into pan. Cover enchiladas with cheese sauce and cilantro. Bake at 375 degrees until bubbly.

Delores Taylor, Class of 1997

Chicken Casserole

½ cup chopped onion
1 cup chopped celery
1 tablespoon margarine
1 cup sliced mushrooms
1 (10¾ ounce) can of
   chicken soup,
   undiluted
1¼ cups sour cream
1 (2 ounce) jar pimiento,
   drained

4-5 cups cubed cooked
   chicken
1¼ cups cooked noodles
1 cup cooked English
   peas
⅔ cup seasoned bread
   crumbs
1 small can sliced water
   chestnuts
¼ cup almonds

TOPPING

1⅔ cups finely crushed Ritz
   crackers
½ cup melted butter

3 teaspoons poppy seeds,
   optional
¼ cup almonds

Sauté onion and celery in margarine until wilted. Add mushrooms. Stir in soup, sour cream and pimiento. Mix well and set aside. Combine chicken, noodles, peas, bread crumbs, water chestnuts and almonds. Mix well. Stir in soup mixture and pour into greased 3-quart casserole dish. Toss crackers in butter. Stir in poppy seeds. Spread over casserole. Sprinkle with almonds. Bake at 350 degrees for 30 minutes.

Yield: 8 to 10 servings

Jean Webb, Class of 1993

"I didn't prepare for retirement. I was a workaholic. I wasn't ready for doing nothing. The LIFE classes filled a void that I needed badly filled. I had broken my ankle more than once and was sort of forced to retire. I wasn't prepared for it on any level. Now I am empowered to do whatever I think I can do."

Shirley Minor,
Class of 1992

Spicy Chicken Wings

4	pounds chicken wings	½	cup hot pepper sauce
	Oil	2	tablespoons cider
½	cup butter, melted		vinegar

Cut wings into three pieces, discarding wing tips. Fry chicken in hot oil until crisp and juices run clear, 5 to 7 minutes for small parts, 6 to 8 minutes for drumettes. Combine butter, hot pepper sauce and vinegar in bowl. Add chicken and toss to coat. Drain. Serve with carrots, celery and blue cheese dressing.

Yield: about 3 dozen

Merle Smith, Class of 1998

"I had just been forced to take what I felt was an early retirement. I decided to sign up for LIFE class to satisfy my wife. Not only did I finish the class, but I saw that I was needed in many ways in the community. I became a Senior Link Hotline volunteer with Senior Leaders and eventually was hired as the Hotline Coordinator. I think retirement is hard for men. LIFE class changes all that."

Chris Glass,
Class of 1996

Chicken Spaghetti

4-5	pounds chicken	1	cup mushrooms
12	ounces spaghetti	1	(14½ ounce) can
	noodles		tomatoes
4	small onions, chopped	1	pound grated cheese
2	green peppers, chopped		

Cook, debone and chop chicken, reserving 1 cup of broth. Cook spaghetti noodles until tender. Drain and set aside. Sauté onions in reserved broth. Combine chicken, onion, peppers, mushrooms, tomatoes and spaghetti. Mix together and add cheese. Pour into casserole dish and bake at 350 degrees for 45 minutes.

Yield: 8 to 10 servings

Gayle Toland, Class of 1995

Italian Chicken Tetrazini

½	pound macaroni or other noodles	1	(10 ounce) can cream of chicken soup
½	cup chopped onion	1	soup can milk
½	cup chopped celery	2	cups precooked chicken
3	tablespoons margarine		

Cook noodles, drain and set aside. Sauté onion and celery in margarine. When tender, add soup, milk and chicken. Let simmer for approximately 7 minutes. Pour noodles into baking dish. Top with sauce. Bake at 350 degrees for 15 minutes. Serve warm.

Theresa Hudson, Class of 1992

Coke 'n Chicken

1	whole fryer chicken, cut up	1	cup Coke
1	cup catsup		Salt and pepper to taste

In a large saucepan, mix together all ingredients and bring to boil. Reduce heat and simmer until tender, stirring occasionally.

Note: You can vary this recipe by using lemon juice, orange juice, hot sauce or Worcestershire sauce.

Shirley Minor, Class of 1992

I discovered this recipe when I was at Girl Scout camp with my daughters. It is easy to make over a fire or stove. It's filling, and good too. Great for something quick to cook for a lot of hungry girls.

"Because of LIFE class, I am able to communicate my feelings, thoughts and opinions to family, doctors, friends, brothers and sisters. They always made decisions for me. I needed to make up my own mind, say no when I needed to. I felt a lot of growth. I make my own direction."

Geneva Burns, Class of 1996

Mandarin Tuna and Cashews

3 tablespoons oil	1 cup celery, chopped
1 green pepper, chopped	1 (5 ounce) can water
½ cup onion, diced	chestnuts, sliced
1 clove garlic, minced	1 (13 ounce) can tuna,
¾ cup dry roasted	drained
cashews, whole	

SEASONING SAUCE

1 tablespoon oil	3 tablespoons granulated
¼ cup sherry	sugar
1 tablespoon cornstarch	1 tablespoon white vinegar
3 tablespoons soy sauce	¼ teaspoon ground ginger
3 tablespoons water	

Heat oil on high in large skillet or wok until hot. Add green pepper, onions, garlic, cashews, celery and water chestnuts. Stir fry for 3 to 5 minutes. In a bowl, mix together all ingredients for seasoning sauce and set aside. Reduce heat to medium and add tuna and seasoning sauce to stir fry. Stir and heat thoroughly. Serve with rice or crisp Chinese noodles.

Yield: 4 servings

L. Almarita Johnson, Class of 1993

Queen Helm's Salmon Croquettes

1	(15½ ounce) can salmon	¼	cup milk
½	bell pepper, chopped	2	tablespoons cornmeal
1	small onion, chopped	1	egg
1	celery stalk	3	dashes Worcestershire sauce
6	crushed crackers	2½	cups vegetable oil
⅓	cup all-purpose flour		

Heat oil in frying pan. Remove bone from salmon. In a bowl, mix salmon with remaining ingredients. Mold into patties. Place in hot oil and fry until golden brown on both sides.

Yield: 8 servings

Merle Helms Smith, Class of 1998

When I was growing up, Friday was a special day at my house. It was Daddy's payday and salmon croquette day. Due to it being the end of the week, the pantry was always scarce on Fridays. The family consisted of 8 hungry children and 2 adults to feed. Mother would always keep a can of salmon or mackerel on the pantry shelf for those emergency meal days. It seemed she could feed an army with one can of salmon. The menu consisted of salmon or mackerel croquettes, rice or creamed potatoes, English peas, biscuits and sheet cake with a vanilla glaze on top. This seemed to be the most delicious meal in the world. When I began to raise my own family, and experienced scarce cupboard Fridays, I prepared the same meal. They too felt this was the best dinner in the world.

As leaders, if we can give hope to those who have lost it, we have done our job.

Sizzled Salmon with Chopped Tomatoes and Mint

1	pound salmon fillets, skin removed	2	tablespoons finely minced fresh mint
¼	cup orange juice	⅛	fresh grated orange rind
1	cup chopped tomatoes	2	teaspoons olive oil
			Chilled orange section

Place salmon in dish with orange juice. Cover and marinate for 10 minutes. In a small bowl, combine tomatoes, mint and orange rind. Set aside. Heat oil in a nonstick skillet. Add salmon and orange juice, sautéing approximately 4 minutes on each side until browned on outside and cooked through. Transfer to serving platter. Top with tomato mixture and garnish with orange sections. Serve hot.

Dorothy Pruitt, Class of 1995

Homemade Grilled Fish Marinade

1	fish fillet	2	tablespoons brown sugar
½	cup soy sauce		
¼	cup water	2	teaspoons minced garlic
¼	chicken bouillon cube	½	teaspoon ground ginger

Set fish in dish. Combine remaining ingredients. Marinate fish for 30 minutes. Grill fish and serve.

Note: You can prepare the marinade and freeze ahead.

Bill Ramsey, Friend of Senior Leaders

Barbecued Shrimp

1¼	pounds fresh shrimp, unpeeled	2	tablespoons cracked black pepper
3	stalks celery with leaves very coarsely chopped	1	tablespoon Worcestershire sauce
1	clove garlic, chopped	1½	teaspoons hot sauce
2	lemons, halved		Lemon wedge
½	cup butter, cut into cubes		

Live as though you will live to be 100, but enjoy today as if it is your last day.

Wash shrimp thoroughly and place in a very large and shallow pan. Add celery and garlic. Squeeze juice from 2 lemons over top. Dot shrimp with butter and sprinkle with remaining ingredients except lemon wedge. Place shrimp under broiler until butter melts and shrimp starts to turn pink, about 5 minutes. Stir several times while cooking. When all shrimp are slightly pink, reduce temperature to 350 degrees. Bake for 15 to 20 minutes or until done, stirring often. Do not overcook or shrimp will become mushy. Taste for doneness. Garnish with lemon wedge.

Note: Flavor improves if shrimp are cooked ahead of time and then reheated, but do not overcook.

Yield: 2 servings

Jane Ramsey, Friend of Senior Leaders

This is a favorite with the adults in my family. We usually enjoy this menu when the girls are at camp or on New Year's Eve. It is very good served with garlic bread. The recipe can easily be increased to please your taste. Just don't put too many shrimp overlaid in the pan. I enjoy the leftovers the next morning.

China Boy 15 Minute Tuna Casserole

2	cups China Boy rice noodles	1	tablespoon instant minced onion
1	can cream of mushroom soup	½	cup cashews, slivered
1	(8 ounce) can China Boy sliced Waterboy chestnuts, drained	1	cup sliced celery
		¼	cup water
		1	(6½ ounce) can tuna, drained
			Almonds or peanuts

Mix 1 cup noodles with remaining ingredients. Spoon into baking dish. Cover with 1 cup noodles. Sprinkle with nuts. Bake at 375 degrees for 15 minutes. After baking, garnish with Mandarin orange slices, pineapple chunks or slices of fresh peaches.

Yield: 4 servings

Louise Fowler, Friend of Senior Leaders

Egg and Cheese Casserole

7	eggs, beaten	6	tablespoons butter
1	cup milk	½	cup all-purpose flour
2	teaspoons granulated sugar	4	ounces cream cheese
1	teaspoon baking powder	1	pound Muenster or Jack cheese, shredded or ½ pound each

Mix together all ingredients. Pour into 9 x 13 inch greased pan. Bake at 325 degrees for 45 minutes. This recipe may be prepared the night before and refrigerated.

Note: By folding cream cheese into milk gradually, you can avoid lumping.

Yield: 8 servings

Terry Adams, Friend of Senior Leaders

Baked Fettuccini

1 pound fettuccini	2 tablespoons bread
⅓ cup butter	crumbs
1 cup grated Parmesan	1 cup shredded
cheese	mozzarella cheese
Salt and pepper to taste	1 cup shrimp or ham, cut
	in strips

Cook fettuccini for 15 minutes in boiling, salted water. Drain, reserving 2 tablespoons of liquid. Add ½ butter, ½ cup Parmesan cheese, reserved liquid and pepper. Sprinkle bottom of a greased baking dish with 1 tablespoon bread crumbs. Layer ½ fettuccini, mozzarella cheese and then shrimp or ham. Cover with remaining fettuccini and dot with butter. Sprinkle with remaining Parmesan cheese and bread crumbs. Bake at 350 degrees until golden brown.

Mary Ann Fox, Class of 1994

My dream for 5 years from now is to continue to be driving.

Brown Rice
Black Bean Burrito

1 tablespoon vegetable oil	1 (13 ounce) can whole
1 medium onion,	kernel corn, drained
chopped	6 (10 inch) tortillas
2 cloves garlic, minced	¾ cup shredded Cheddar
2 teaspoons chili powder	cheese
1 teaspoon cumin	6 green onions, chopped
3 cups cooked brown rice	¼ cup yogurt, optional
1 (15 ounce) can black	Prepared salsa
beans, rinsed and	
drained	

In a large skillet, heat oil over medium-high heat until hot. Add onion, garlic, chili powder and cumin. Sauté 3 to 5 minutes until onion is tender. Add rice, beans and corn. Cook, stirring 2 to 3 minutes until mixture is thoroughly heated. Remove from heat. Spoon ½ cup of rice mixture into center of tortilla. Top each with cheese, green onion, yogurt and salsa. Roll tortillas and serve.

Mattie Lindsey, Class of 2000

Spicy Vegetarian Tamales

You're never too
old to fall in love.

DOUGH

¼ (8 ounce) package dried
  corn husks, 7 x 10
  inches
2½ cups masa harina or
  corn flour
2½ cups water

2½ tablespoons safflower or
  canola oil
1 tablespoon reduced-salt
  soy sauce
1 teaspoon garlic powder

FILLING

2 cups Zesty Crockpot
  Pinto Beans
  (see Veggies)
½ small onion, chopped
⅛ teaspoon cayenne

2½ teaspoons chili powder
2 teaspoons onion powder
½ teaspoon garlic powder
½ teaspoon dried oregano

Soak corn husks in cold water until softened. Separate and drain. Set aside. In a large bowl, mix together remaining dough ingredients with a spoon until smooth. Set aside. In a medium bowl, mix together all filling ingredients. Set aside. Place one corn husk in the palm of hand. Drop 2 heaping tablespoons of dough in center of husk. Drop 1 heaping tablespoon of filling on top of dough. Bring sides of the husk over the filling and dough. Turn down flaps, forming an envelope. Place another husk over the flaps and fold over to keep filling from coming out while steaming. Pour 4 cups water into the bottom of a vegetable steamer. Lay tamales in 2 or 3 overlapping layers in steamer basket. Cover and cook over medium heat until boiling. Reduce heat and simmer for 30 minutes. Serve hot.

Josie Buckner, Class of 1992

Grilled Vegetable Sandwich

2	tablespoons olive oil	1	small sweet onion, sliced ¼ inch
1	clove garlic, crushed		
	Salt and pepper to taste	1	(1 pound) loaf Italian or French bread cut length wise
1	small eggplant, trimmed and quartered		
1	medium yellow squash, trimmed and sliced length wise	½	cup pasta sauce
		½	cup shredded provolone cheese
1	large red bell pepper, cut in 1 inch strips	6	fresh basil leaves, shredded

Heat grill until hot. Combine olive oil, garlic, salt and pepper. Lightly brush vegetable slices with oil mixture. Grill vegetables 3 to 5 minutes per side until tender. Set aside. Heat broiler. Spread pasta sauce evenly on one half of bread. Sprinkle cheese evenly over sauce. Place cheese topped bread under broiler until cheese melts, about 1 to 2 minutes. Sprinkle with basil. Arrange vegetables on melted cheese. Top with remaining bread half. Cut into serving size pieces. Serve with additional pasta sauce if desired.

Yield: 4 servings

Merle Smith, Class of 1998

Blessed are those who grow old together — be they married, friends, or neighbors.

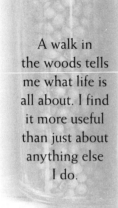

A walk in the woods tells me what life is all about. I find it more useful than just about anything else I do.

Macaroni and Cheese

12	ounce package macaroni	2	tablespoons granulated
1	pound mild cheese		sugar
4	eggs	½	pint half-and-half or
	Salt to taste		milk

Cook macaroni in salted water until tender. Drain. In 2-quart baking dish, layer ½ macaroni and ½ cheese. Repeat. In separate bowl, mix eggs, salt, sugar and half-and-half. Pour over macaroni and cheese. Add more half-and-half if needed to cover. Bake at 350 degrees until bubbly and thick, about 30 minutes.

Note: Onion may be added to liquid mixture if desired.

Josie Buckner, Class of 1992

Cheddar Cheese Casserole

½	cup chopped onion	1	(4 ounce) package
2	tablespoons margarine		shredded sharp
1	(10¾ ounce) can cream		Cheddar cheese
	of celery soup	¼	cup grated Parmesan
⅓	cup milk		cheese
2	cups noodles, cooked	2	tablespoons chopped
	and drained		pimiento
1	(6 ounce) can tuna,	2	tablespoons sliced
	drained and flaked		mushrooms

Sauté onion in margarine. Add soup and milk. Stir in remaining ingredients except ½ cup Cheddar cheese. Pour into 1-quart casserole dish. Bake at 350 degrees for 30 minutes. Remove from oven and top with remaining cheese. Bake in oven until cheese melts.

Wanda Hogg, Class of 1995

Veggies and Other Tasty Sides

The Good Ole Days

Times have certainly changed since I was a little girl. I was born in the depression era. We were farmers back when farms were small and provided a living for a family. Cotton was the money crop. Corn was for grinding into cornmeal to make cornbread, which was a staple. Corn along with hay provided food for the livestock.

The mules were used to till the soil, pigs for food, and the cows for milk and butter. We planted pumpkins and all kinds of beans and field peas in the cornfield so they could grow up the cornstalks for support. We usually grew enough of these to last the winter. We had fruit trees to provide fruit for canning, drying and eating fresh when it was in season.

We grew sugar cane for making molasses. My father had a molasses mill and made molasses for others as well as ourselves. My father would carry buckets of molasses to town (Fayetteville, TN) to sell to earn some money, one thing that we couldn't grow on the farm. Sometimes he brought it all back because he found no one with money to buy it. We raised chickens for eggs. Most of the eggs we swapped at the "rolling store" or "peddler" for coffee, sugar, flour and other things we couldn't grow.

We looked forward to spring. We could go out foraging for wild greens. Poke sallet and greens we called "creasy sallet." These were a welcome change to our winter diet. Country children learned early on how to recognize edible wild food. As poor as we were, we fared better than city folk. At least we could make our own soup without waiting in line at a soup kitchen.

In the spring we planted Irish potatoes and sweet potatoes. Irish potatoes were ready to eat by late spring. The sweet potatoes matured later and were a good storage potato for the winter.

The vegetable garden yielded from early spring until frost. Mother planted lettuce, radishes and onions as soon as the ground was warm. They matured fast, and we could begin eating them while they were quite small on up until they went to seed. Tomatoes, okra, squash, English Peas, cucumbers and others were planted after all danger of frost had passed. Mother grew 3 special vegetables that I will never forget - early sweet corn, sweet white multiplying onions, and Kentucky wonder beans. The early sweet corn was better than any I have eaten since. Picked and cooked within the same morning, the taste was heavenly.

The changing of the seasons was so pronounced. I can still close my eyes and see the wild bush honeysuckle in the spring. There were shades of pink growing in masses along the hillside of "Teal Holler." The fragrance was heavenly.

Think these were the "good ole days?" Don't you believe it. I just choose to remember the "good" part of the "ole days."

Jennie Morring, Class of 1992

Eggplant Surprise

1	large eggplant		Salt and pepper to taste
1	(10¾ ounce) can mushroom soup	1	egg, beaten
1½	cups bread crumbs	3	tablespoons butter
1	cup grated Cheddar cheese	½	cup bread crumbs for topping

Peel and cut eggplant. Cook and drain. Mash into small pieces. Add remaining ingredients. Mix well. Place in buttered casserole dish and top with bread crumbs. Bake at 350 degrees until bubbly.

Mary Jo Williams, Friend of Senior Leaders

Baked Eggplant

1	large eggplant	⅓	cup bread crumbs
1	egg, beaten	½	cup Cheddar cheese
1	onion, chopped		Salt and pepper to taste
½	cup butter		

Cube eggplant. Cook until tender. Drain. Add egg, onion, butter, bread crumbs and cheese. Season with salt and pepper. Bake at 350 degrees for 30 minutes.

Anne Weathers, Class of 1995

"I kept telling myself I'm older now and must accept some things. But I came to leadership class where discussions on self-esteem helped me hold my head up. I found out I don't have to accept things because I'm older. I still can do and Lord knows I can still think for myself."

Lois Fluornoy, Class of 1992

Italian Eggplant Parmesan

¼ cup all-purpose flour
¼ cup cornmeal
1 medium eggplant, unpeeled and sliced to ½ inch

1 egg, beaten
Salt and pepper to taste
Parmesan cheese

Combine flour and cornmeal. Dip eggplant slices in egg then flour mixture. Place in pan of tepid oil and sprinkle over salt and pepper to taste. Fry until brown on both sides. Drain on paper towel. Sprinkle Parmesan over top and serve.

Theresa Hudson, Class of 1992

I find that I enjoy spending time with my grandchildren in a way that I never felt with my children. At first I felt guilty. Then I realized, hey, this is one of the rewards of aging — hanging out with grandchildren, laughing, fishing, messing with the computer — and not worrying every day about their future.

Spinach Casserole

2 (14 ounce) cans spinach, drained
2 eggs, beaten
1 onion, chopped
½ cup mayonnaise

1 (10¾ ounce) can mushroom soup
1 cup grated cheese
Buttered bread crumbs

Mix all ingredients except bread crumbs. Pour into greased casserole dish. Top with bread crumbs or more cheese. Bake at 350 degrees for 45 minutes.

Note: I like to use celery soup in place of mushroom. This recipe also can be made with broccoli.

Evelyn Cornelius, Class of 1993

Potato Casserole I

CASSEROLE

3	cups sweet potatoes, cut in chunks	2	eggs, beaten
1	cup granulated sugar	½	stick butter, melted
½	teaspoon salt	½	cup milk
		½	teaspoon vanilla

TOPPING

1	cup brown sugar	⅓	cup all-purpose flour
⅓	stick butter	1	cup chopped nuts

Mix together first 7 ingredients. Pour into 2 quart casserole dish. Combine brown sugar, butter and flour. Mix in nuts. Place topping over mixture and bake at 350 degrees for 35 minutes.

Martin Stevenson, Class of 1995

This recipe was given to me by my wife's cousin's husband in Nashville, Tennessee. He brought it to a Thanksgiving get-together and said it was an ideal recipe for a man to do. It makes a great covered dish dinner or pot luck supper.

Potato Casserole II

CASSEROLE

1	package frozen hash brown potatoes, thawed	1	(10 ounce) can cream of chicken, celery or mushroom soup
2	cups shredded cheese	2	cups sour cream
½	cup chopped onion	1	teaspoon salt
		1	teaspoon pepper
		½	cup melted margarine

TOPPING

½	cup butter	2	cups crushed corn flakes

Combine ingredients and pour into casserole dish. Combine butter and corn flakes. Sprinkle over mixture. Bake at 350 degrees for 1 hour.

Jane Ramsey, Friend of Senior Leaders

Once my teacher asked, "How old will each of you be at the turn of the century?" My thought was, "I'll be dead." Imagine my surprise to find that I am still living. I plan to live to be 100.

Mashed Potato Salad

"If you live long enough, you too will experience the challenges of aging."

4-5	medium potatoes, peeled and quartered	2	tablespoons vinegar
¼	cup of milk	½	cup salad dressing (not mayonnaise)
½	cup butter	3	hard-boiled eggs, chopped
	Additional seasoning, optional	1	tablespoon prepared mustard
¼	cup minced onion		Salt and pepper to taste
¼	cup minced sweet pickles		

Peel and quarter potatoes. Boil potatoes until tender and mash in a large bowl. Blend in milk, butter and seasoning. To potato mixture, add minced onion, sweet pickles, vinegar and salad dressing. Fold in ⅔ of chopped eggs. Stir in prepared mustard. Add salt and pepper to taste. Garnish with remaining ⅓ chopped eggs. This is wonderful hot or cold.

Nelda Grimes, Class of 1992

New Potatoes with Roasted Garlic

6	large garlic cloves, chopped	1	tablespoon capers
2	tablespoons margarine	¼	teaspoon salt
1½	pounds new potatoes, quartered	¼	teaspoon freshly ground pepper
2	tablespoons water	¼	teaspoon grated lemon peel
2	tablespoons chopped parsley		

Combine garlic and margarine in a microwave safe bowl. Partially cover and microwave for 2 minutes. Place potatoes and water in 12 x 7 inch microwave safe dish. Add garlic mixture and mix well. Partially cover and microwave for 8 minutes or until tender. Stir in remaining ingredients.

Yield: 4 servings

Evelyn Cornelius, Class of 1993

Sweet Potato Pudding

Sweet potatoes   Marshmallows
Sugar to taste

Boil potatoes until tender. Mix in sugar to taste. Pour into pie dish. Cover with marshmallows and bake at 350 degrees for 10 minutes.

Cordelia Montgomery, Class of 1995

This is a classic old-time recipe. No measurements are needed.

Sweet Potato Pond

3   large sweet potatoes
4   tablespoons butter
1½ cups granulated sugar
3   large eggs
1   (14 ounce) can
    evaporated milk

½   teaspoon ground
    cinnamon
½   teaspoon ground allspice
½   teaspoon nutmeg
1   teaspoon vanilla
½   teaspoon lemon extract

Boil sweet potatoes until tender. Add butter, sugar, eggs and milk. Mix well. Add remaining ingredients. Beat well. Drop filling onto a baking sheet and shape into a pond. Bake at 350 degrees for 30 to 40 minutes. Let cool. Top with whipped topping and serve.

Edna Burton, Class of 1994

When my grandmother turned 76, we had a birthday cake for her with all 76 candles on the cake. Looking at all those candles, I thought, she must be really old. But when I looked at her face in the candle glow, she seemed timeless, ageless. I could not imagine what life would be without her.

B.J.'s Sweet Potato Casserole

CASSEROLE

4	cups sweet potatoes	2	eggs, beaten
½	cup granulated sugar	⅓	cup milk
½	cup margarine	2	teaspoons vanilla

TOPPING

½	cup margarine	½	cup all-purpose flour or
1⅓	cups brown sugar		quick oats
		1	cup chopped pecans

Boil, peel and mash potatoes. Mix in sugar, margarine and eggs. Add milk and vanilla. Pour mixture into large baking dish. For topping, melt margarine and mix in remaining ingredients. Sprinkle over potato mixture. Bake at 350 degrees for 25 minutes.

B.J. Glass, Class of 1996

This recipe has always been a favorite at potluck celebrations at the Senior Leaders office.

Microwave
Sweet Vidalia Onions

1	Vidalia onion, peeled	1	chicken or beef bouillon cube

Carve out hole in top of onion. Insert bouillon cube. Microwave 3 to 4 minutes per onion.

Gayle Toland, Class of 1995

Berks County Potato Filling

6	medium potatoes	1½	cups milk
1	medium onion, diced	2	teaspoons salt
½	cup finely minced celery	⅛	teaspoon pepper
2	tablespoons butter	2	tablespoons minced
3	slices bread, French or		parsley
	Vienna	1	egg, beaten

Peel potatoes and cook in lightly salted water until soft. In a saucepan, brown onion and celery in butter. Tear bread into small pieces and set aside. In a large bowl, mash cooked potatoes. Add sautéed onion and celery, bread, ½ cup milk, salt, pepper and parsley. Beat by hand until smooth. Add egg and remaining milk. Beat again until blended. Turn into greased casserole dish and bake at 350 degrees for 1½ hours.

Yield: 8 servings

Bobbie Thompson, Class of 1997

Cabbage Rolls

1	large head cabbage	1	egg
1	pound ground beef	1	clove garlic, pressed
½	pound sausage		Salt and pepper to taste
1	cup cooked rice	2	tablespoons paprika
1	medium onion, diced	1	(16 ounce) can sauerkraut

Core cabbage and place head in boiling water for 3 minutes. Gently pull off each leaf and trim thick, center vein. Mix ground beef, sausage, rice, onion, egg, garlic, salt and pepper. Lay out cabbage leaves one at a time filling each with 1 large spoonful of meat mixture. Roll leaves and tuck edges. Arrange rolls in large pan or baking dish. Sprinkle 1 tablespoon paprika over rolls. Cover with sauerkraut. Sprinkle with remaining paprika. Add water until ½ covered. Bake at 350 degrees for 30 to 45 minutes.

Jack Range, Friend of Senior Leaders

Lemon Rice with Pecans

In LIFE class,
I became
reconnected to
the creative spirit
inside me that
I had lost through
years of raising
children and care
giving. A whole
new world was
open to me. I wake
up everyday
thinking about
quilts, painting —
you name it.

1	tablespoon butter	¼	cup fresh lemon juice
⅓	cup minced onion	1	lemon rind, grated
1	cup uncooked long grain white rice	¼	cup chopped pecans or toasted almonds
1¾	cups chicken stock		

In a medium sauce pan, melt butter and sauté onion over medium heat for 5 minutes or until translucent, but not browned. Blend in rice and stir until all grains are coated. Add stock, lemon juice and lemon rind. Bring to boil. Reduce heat, cover and simmer 20 minutes, or until liquid is absorbed. Stir in pecans and serve immediately.

Yield: 6 servings

Ivan L. Richards, Class of 1993

This is one of my favorite dishes. My wife makes it often since it is not only healthy and tasty, but it is also quick and easy!

Zucchini Frittata

2	cups thinly sliced zucchini	2	tablespoons olive oil
1	clove garlic, crushed	8	eggs, beaten
3	scallions, including tops, sliced	¾	cup grated Parmesan cheese
4	tablespoons chopped fresh parsley	¼	teaspoon salt
		¼	teaspoon pepper

Preheat oven to 350 degrees. In a large skillet, sauté zucchini, garlic, scallions and parsley in olive oil over medium heat. Stir vegetables lightly for 3 to 5 minutes. Remove from heat and add eggs, cheese, salt and pepper. Pour mixture into greased 9-inch square pan and bake. Slice into squares and serve immediately.

Yield: 8 servings

Shoghig "Sunny" Ross,
Senior Leaders Board of Directors

Baked Squash Casserole

2 pounds yellow squash, sliced	½ teaspoon hot sauce
¼ cup chopped onion	Salt and pepper to taste
2 eggs	½ cup melted butter
2 teaspoons dried parsley	1½ cups bread crumbs

Boil squash until tender. Drain. Add onion, eggs and seasonings. Mix until well blended. Pour into a buttered casserole dish. Mix butter and crumbs. Sprinkle over squash mixture. Bake at 350 degrees for 30 minutes.

Theresa Hudson, Class of 1992

Cheesed Cauliflower

1 fresh, medium cauliflower head	2 teaspoons prepared mustard
Salt to taste	¾ cup sharp processed cheese
½ cup mayonnaise	

Remove leaves and trim base of cauliflower. Wash. Cook whole in boiling salted water 15 to 20 minutes or until tender. Drain. Place on ungreased shallow baking dish. Sprinkle with salt. Mix together mayonnaise and prepared mustard. Spread over cauliflower. Top with cheese. Bake at 375 degrees for 10 minutes or until cheese has melted.

Lois Hawks, LIFE Class 2000

This is highly recommended by my two oldest granddaughters who fight over this one. It's a great way to get the kids to try cauliflower.

When I came to LIFE class, I had just retired. I thought I was empowered. After all, I had been active in unions and other advocacy organizations. I learned so much from LIFE class that I decided to become a LIFE trainer. I want all seniors to have our fondest dream — to remain independent and at home.

Merle Smith, Class of 1998

Maine Woods Baked Beans

Connecting with the simple and little things in life keeps my heart in the right place. The sweet fragrance of a rose, my dog's nose pressed against the window, the feeling of dough beneath my fingers, the sound of my grandsons' giggle. Oh how rich life can be.

1	pound White Northern beans	1	cup ketchup
1½	teaspoons salt	1	cup sorghum molasses
2	tablespoons dry mustard	½	cup brown sugar, packed
1	large yellow onion, finely chopped	1	(3 or 4 inch) square lean salt or sugar cured meat, sliced with skins on

Soak washed beans overnight in plenty of water. In morning, drain reserving liquid. Add fresh water and bring to boil. Simmer until you can take a spoonful of beans out, blow on them, and the skins will curl up. Pour beans in oven proof pot. Add remaining ingredients except meat. Bury meat in middle of beans. Cover and bake at 350 degrees for 3 to 5 hours. Watch beans and add reserved liquid when needed. Stir often.

Nelda Grimes, Class of 1992

The woman who gave this recipe to me used a wood stove and it took about 7 hours to cook. We would take to the woods while it would cook.

Zesty Crockpot Pinto Beans

3	cups dry pinto beans	2	bay leaves
8	cups water	1	tablespoon reduced-salt soy sauce
1	large onion, chopped		
2	celery stalks, chopped	1	teaspoon Vegit or other salt substitute
½	red or green bell pepper, chopped	4	cups boiling water
1	large tomato, chopped		

Bring beans and 8 cups water to a boil in a large pot. Boil for 10 minutes. Let beans soak in water until cool or overnight. Drain and rinse beans well. Put beans into crockpot. Stir in remaining ingredients. Cover and cook on high for 12 to 16 hours. Serve hot.

Josie Buckner, Class of 1992

Baked Beans

1	small onion, chopped	¼	cup ketchup
1	medium green pepper, chopped	2	tablespoons mustard
1	(15 ounce) can pork and beans	2	tablespoons packed brown sugar or molasses
1	(15 ounce) can red or kidney beans	1	tablespoon Worcestershire sauce
1	small can pineapple chunks, drained	¼	cup Bar-B-Que sauce

Lightly sauté onion and green pepper. Mix together all ingredients in a 3-quart baking dish. Bake at 325 degrees for 1 hour.

Note: Flat, big pans tend to cook more quickly and should cook for approximately 45 minutes.

Heather Baugus, Honorary Class of 1998

This recipe is one of my mother's signature dishes. Though it turns out delicious when following this recipe, she always seems to have the touch to make it that much better — sometimes adding a little more here and a little less there. I typically do not like baked beans, but when my mother makes this for a special occasion, I can't resist.

"It empowered me to be the person I know myself to be, even at the age I am, because age doesn't matter. What matters is desire and determination. The LIFE class allowed me to express the desire and gave me the determination to reach for my dreams."

Betty Halstead, Class of 1995

Spinach Rice

2	cups rice, cooked	1	cup minced parsley
2	cups chicken broth	2	cups fresh spinach
2	cups water		Olive oil
1	cup minced green onions	1	cup walnuts, optional
			Salt and pepper to taste

Cook rice in broth and water. Sauté onions, parsley and spinach in olive oil until wilted. Mix with rice mixture. Add walnuts and salt and pepper to taste.

Nelda Grimes, Class of 1992

Peas 'n' Rice

1 cup pigeon peas or crowder peas, dried	Dash onion salt
1 large smoked ham hock	Black pepper to taste
2 slices fat back	1 basil leaf, crushed
1 medium onion, sliced	1 ounce pepper sauce
	1 cup rice

Soak peas overnight. Boil ham hock in water until ¾ done, then add soaked, drained peas. Fry fat back until brown, pour off fat. Lightly sauté onion. In a large pot, combine fat back, sautéed onion, onion salt, pepper, basil and peas. Pour in pepper sauce. Add rice and stir well. Cook at 350 degrees for 45 minutes or until peas and rice are done.

Mary Bonner, Class of 1995

Green Bean Casserole

2 (9 ounce) packages frozen cut green beans, thawed and drained	1 (10¾ ounce) can condensed cream of mushroom soup
¾ cup milk	¼ teaspoon ground black pepper
	1 (2.8 ounce) can French-fried onions

In a medium bowl, combine beans, milk, soup, pepper and ½ can of fried onions. Pour into 2-quart casserole dish. Bake uncovered at 350 degrees for 30 minutes. Top with remaining fried onions. Bake for 5 minutes or until onions are golden brown.

Yield: 6 servings

Frances Taylor, Class of 1997
Mignon Boals, Class of 1994

Nelda's Healthy Green Beans

2	pounds green beans, fresh or frozen	1	tablespoon olive oil
1	small onion, chopped	¼	teaspoon garlic powder
		1	teaspoon lemon pepper

Boil green beans for 8 to 10 minutes. Drain and set aside. Sauté onion in olive oil until yellow, but not brown. Add garlic powder and lemon pepper. Toss in green beans.

Yield: 8 servings

Nelda Grimes, Class of 1992

Fresh Colorful Vegetable Medley

2	cups peeled and chopped turnips	2	cups peeled and chopped tomatoes
2	tablespoons olive oil	2	cups fresh corn from cob
2	cups chopped onion	1	teaspoon chopped fresh basil, optional
2	cloves garlic, minced		Salt and pepper to taste

Drop turnip greens in boiling water. Cook for 10 minutes until almost tender. Drain. In oil, sauté onion 5 minutes. Add garlic. Cook 2 minutes, careful not to brown. Add tomatoes, turnips and corn. Simmer gently for 5 minutes until juices begin to evaporate and flavors mix. Add basil, salt and pepper.

Nelda Grimes, Class of 1992

Corn Pudding

2	(16 ounce) cans whole kernel corn	1	cup evaporated milk
2	(16 ounce) cans cream style corn	1	teaspoon cinnamon
		1	teaspoon black pepper
2	eggs	1	packet sugar substitute or 1 tablespoon granulated sugar
½	stick butter, melted		
½	cup all-purpose flour		

Drain whole kernel corn. Mix together all ingredients. Bake uncovered at 350 degrees for 30 to 40 minutes until lightly browned on top.

Mary Bonner, Class of 1995

Corn Bread Casserole

1	(15¼ ounce) can whole kernel corn, drained	1	egg, beaten
1	(14¾ ounce) can cream style corn	2	tablespoons butter, melted
1	(8½ ounce) package cornbread mix	¼	teaspoon garlic powder
		¼	teaspoon paprika

In a large bowl, combine all ingredients. Pour into greased 11 x 7 x 2 inch baking dish. Bake, uncovered, at 400 degrees for 25 to 30 minutes or until top and edges are golden brown.

Yield: 4 to 6 servings

Lucille Willis, Friend of Senior Leaders

Sunday Morning Grits

½	pound sausage	½	cup Parmesan or hoop cheese
½	stick butter		Dash cayenne pepper
6	cups cooked grits		Dash salt
4	eggs, beaten		Paprika
2	cups milk		

Preheat oven to 375 degrees. Grease large casserole dish with shortening and set aside. Sauté sausage in butter and drain well. In a large bowl, thoroughly mix sausage, grits, eggs, milk, cheese, pepper and salt. Pour into casserole dish. Bake for 25 to 30 minutes. Sprinkle with paprika and serve.

Yield: 8 to 10 servings

Lillie Nelson, Class of 1992

This recipe was always doubled by adding more grits and milk. We all loved it and still do. It is served for Christmas morning brunch.

As we age, we learn to continue doing for ourselves, even when others offer to help us because, after all, we're getting old. Dependency doesn't happen overnight. It happens one step at a time.

Cheese Garlic Grits

1	cup uncooked grits	2	eggs, well beaten
1½	cups Cheddar cheese	1	small garlic clove, minced
½	cup butter		
½	cup milk		

Preheat oven to 350 degrees. Prepare grits as directed on package. Stir in remaining ingredients. Cook over low heat until cheese is melted. Pout into 2-quart casserole dish. Bake for 45 to 60 minutes.

Yield: 6 servings

Mike Bilderback, Friend of Senior Leaders

Onion Pie

An interesting experience was after being in the LIFE class, then going to the doctor. I became assertive, and asked questions, and got the information that perhaps I had been a little too intimidated to ask before.

Joe Watson,
Class of 1996

1 cup finely crumbled Ritz crackers	¾ cup milk
½ stick butter, melted	¾ teaspoon salt
2 cups thinly sliced Vidalia onions	Dash of pepper
2 teaspoons butter	¼ cup grated sharp Cheddar cheese
2 eggs	Paprika to taste
	Parsley leaves

Mix cracker crumbs with butter until clear. Do not brown. Spoon into crust. Beat eggs with milk, salt and pepper. Pour over onions. Sprinkle with cheese and paprika. Bake at 350 degrees for 30 minutes or until knife comes out clean. Garnish with parsley.

Yield: 6 to 8 servings

Georgia Bartosch, Class of 1992

There is an onion lover in our family, and when Vidalia onions come on the market we try to make this recipe. He hopes against hope it will be included in the menu when the family gets together for a celebration.

Sour Cream Onion Pie

1 (10 inch) pie crust, baked	1 teaspoon salt
3 cups peeled and sliced onions	2 eggs, well beaten
3 tablespoons melted butter	3 tablespoons all-purpose flour
½ cup milk	3 bacon slices, cooked crisp
1½ cups sour cream	

Bake pie crust and set aside. Sauté onions in butter until lightly brown. Spoon into crust. In a large bowl, mix together milk, 1¼ cups sour cream, salt and eggs. In a small bowl, blend flour and remaining sour cream. Add flour mixture to egg mixture and pour over onions. Bake at 325 degrees for 30 minutes or until firm in center. Garnish with crisp bacon.

Yield: 8 servings

Committee

Southern Cornbread Dressing

1	cup chopped celery	4	cups loaf bread or
¾	cup finely chopped		biscuits, crumbled
	onion	1	tablespoon salt
1	cup water	⅛	teaspoon pepper
6	cups crumbled	4	eggs, beaten
	cornbread	½	cup butter, melted
		2	cups broth

Cook celery and onion in water over low heat until tender. Add to crumbs. Add seasoning. Stir in eggs, butter and enough broth to moisten mix. Pour into greased pan and bake at 400 degrees for about 30 minutes or until brown.

Jane Ramsey, Friend of Senior Leaders

This is how my mother and grandmother made cornbread dressing. It is a rather dry dressing, but it is what I like. I remember well the scent of the mixture before it went into the oven. The use of cornbread truly makes this southern. Typically, in the South, dressing is not used to stuff the turkey.

Recipe for Cooking Poke Sallet

1	cup boiled Poke sallet	1	egg
	leaves, drained*		Potatoes, optional

Wash and remove tough stems of poke sallet. In a pot, place leaves in water and cook until wilted and tender. Drain. In a skillet, heat bacon fat or pork fat. Add leaves. Cook until all water is cooked out. Add egg. Cook until egg is done and combined into sallet. Serve with red onions, cornbread and maybe some white potatoes.

Jennie Morring, Class of 1993

Note: *One quart packed fresh leaves yields 1 cup.

"If you have a dream, if you have things you've even considered doing and aren't doing because you think you are too old, you'd better think again. You don't know what you are throwing away if you don't try. I don't have a college education, but last summer I went on an archaeological dig. I wouldn't take a million dollars for that experience. The best memory as far as I'm concerned is that I proved to myself that even though I'm the age that I am now, I can still do something like this."

Bobbie Thompson, Class of 1997

"Yankee" Dressing

The thing I like most about the age I am now is the freedom to go to bed when I want, eat what I want, get up when I want, and more or less do what I want.

1 loaf stale white bread, crumbled
2 tablespoons sage
   Salt and pepper to taste
1 stick butter
3 medium onions, chopped fine
8 sticks celery, chopped fine
½ cup milk
1 large egg
   Giblets, mushrooms or oysters, optional

Season bread crumbs by tossing with sage, salt and pepper. Sauté onion and celery in butter until tender. Mix together milk and egg. Combine all ingredients and toss until mixed well. Add more milk if needed to make sure all bread is moistened. Stuff into chicken or turkey. Bake according to directions provided on poultry. For variety you can add giblets from turkey or chicken, mushrooms or oysters.

Note: Giblets are made from the liver, gizzard, and neck bones. Boil all together and chop fine.

Shirley Minor, Class of 1992

My 4 daughters love this recipe, even the three who were born in the South.

Did you know there is a basic difference between the way dressing (as in turkey and dressing) is made in the North and the South? People from the North tend to use stale white bread as the base of the dressing, while cooks in the South like to use cornbread as the base of their dressing.

Heavenly Carrots

2	pounds carrots, cut diagonal	1	cup granulated sugar
1	small green pepper, diced	½	cup salad oil
1	medium onion, sliced	¾	cup vinegar
1	(10¾ ounce) can tomato soup	1	teaspoon mustard
		1	teaspoon Worcestershire sauce
			Salt to taste

Boil or steam carrots until tender. Drain and put into 2-quart casserole dish. Layer pepper and onion over carrots. In a large bowl, blend soup, sugar, oil, vinegar, mustard and Worcestershire sauce. Add salt to taste. Pour over top layer. Refrigerate over night.

Helen Page, Class of 1994

Carrot Soufflé

2	cups cooked carrots, lightly salted	1	cup granulated sugar
1	stick butter, melted	1	teaspoon baking powder
2	eggs, well beaten	1	teaspoon cinnamon
3	tablespoons all-purpose flour		

In a large bowl, mash carrots. Add butter and eggs. In a separate bowl, combine dry ingredients. Pour both mixtures into a blender and blend on medium-high for 1 minute. Pour into a 2-quart casserole dish. Bake at 400 degrees for 15 minutes. Decrease temperature to 350 degrees and bake for 45 minutes. Serve hot.

Note: Using a mixer does not work as well as a blender for this recipe. Enjoy!

Evelyn Cornelius, Class of 1993

"It is for me when someone makes it like you are over the hill and you don't know where you are going or where you have been. We just started a class tutoring at my church and a very young educated lady assumed that I could not do the math that the children have. She has been to college and she has a degree behind her, but I told her that I learned my multiplication tables and I can subtract just as well as she can. It is very disturbing when a younger person comes along and counts you out."

Victoria Smith,
Class of 1994

Copper Pennies

"Listen to us. We have something important to say."

2 pounds carrots, scraped and sliced
1 (10¾ ounce) can tomato soup
½ cup salad oil
1 cup granulated sugar
1 teaspoon prepared mustard
1 teaspoon Worcestershire sauce
¾ cup vinegar
1 small bell pepper, sliced
1 medium onion, sliced

Boil carrots in salted water until tender, 3 to 5 minutes. Drain immediately. Mix together soup, oil, sugar, mustard, Worcestershire and vinegar. Layer cooked carrots, onion and peppers in a dish and cover with soup mixture. Refrigerate 12 hours. Serve cold.

Committee

Scalloped Rhubarb

2 (16 ounce) packages frozen rhubarb
¾ cup granulated sugar
1 cup water
¼ cup packed light brown sugar
1 cup chopped onion
½ cup butter
1 (8 ounce) package herb-seasoned stuffing

In a 3-quart saucepan, mix together rhubarb, sugar and water. Bring to boil over high heat. Cover and reduce heat to low. Simmer for 5 minutes. Remove from heat and drain, reserving liquid. Top rhubarb with brown sugar. Sauté onion in butter for 4 minutes. Add 1 cup reserved liquid to stuffing. Toss to combine. Put ½ of rhubarb mixture into a shallow 2-quart casserole dish. Top with ½ stuffing. Repeat. Bake at 350 degrees for 45 minutes.

Helen Lockhart, Class of 1995

Pineapple Cheddar Casserole

1 (20 ounce) can crushed or chunk pineapple	1¼ cups shredded Cheddar cheese
3 tablespoons granulated sugar	1½ cups crushed Ritz crackers
3 tablespoons all-purpose flour	3 tablespoons melted butter

Drain pineapple, reserving juice. Place pineapple in a 2-quart casserole dish. Sprinkle with sugar and flour. Drizzle with 3 tablespoons of juice. Cover with cheese. Top with crackers and butter. Cover and bake at 350 degrees for 15 minutes. Uncover and bake 10 minutes.

Yield: 6 servings

Georgia Bartosch, Class of 1992

White Instant Potatoes

6 servings instant potato flakes	3 tablespoons grated onion
1 egg, beaten	3 tablespoons butter, melted
8 ounces cream cheese	Paprika

Mix instant potatoes as directed on package, omitting butter. Add egg, cream cheese and onion. Mix well. Place in greased 2 quart casserole dish and drizzle with butter. Sprinkle with paprika and bake at 350 degrees for 30 minutes.

Note: This dish works well with fresh potatoes. Simply cook and mash potatoes then prepare as shown above.

Jennie Morring, Class of 1993

Harvard Beets

½	cup granulated sugar	2	(16 ounce) cans diced or
1	tablespoon cornstarch		sliced beets, drained
½	cup water	2	tablespoons butter
¼	cup cider vinegar	1	teaspoon salt
		¼	teaspoon pepper

In a medium saucepan, mix sugar, cornstarch, water and vinegar until blended. Bring to boil, stirring constantly. Decrease heat and simmer 5 minutes. Stir in beets. Remove from heat and cover. Let stand 30 minutes. Just before serving, bring to boil. Stir in butter, salt and pepper. Serve warm.

Yield: 6 servings

Evelyn Cornelius, Class of 1993

Sauces and Spreads

*The most important thing I can do for my children
and grandchildren is to pray for them and share with
them some of my knowledge and wisdom.*

My Grandmother

I was blessed to spend my very early childhood with my maternal grandmother, who owned an apple orchard in Berks County, Pennsylvania. Competition for field hands and pickers at harvest time was stiff, but word of the best cooks in the area was passed around and those farmers had their choice of workers. My grandmother was a widow, but she never wanted for help. I really don't remember, but I have been told she was that kind of cook (Too bad I didn't inherit any of her expertise!). Granny spent half of the night cooking a "sawmill" breakfast. It usually consisted of fried potatoes, potato filling, milk gravy, ham and small donut squares made with sour cream. And there were desserts for breakfast too. Shoo-fly pie (oh, yes there really is such a thing), fried apple pies, crumb cake or cookies. This was served before 4 am and by 9 o'clock we would be on our way to the field with lunch. I can remember carrying funnel cakes, cookies and a favorite drink of the harvesters called Essich Schling. It was made with ice water, sugar, vinegar, baking soda and nutmeg. Doesn't sound too good to me, but they loved it. It was 9 in the morning and Granny still had to cook supper, bake bread and ready up the house. But with all she had to do, my grandmother scrubbed her clothes on a board and boiled them in a copper pot on a wood stove until they were snow white. The house was spic and span too! Granny taught me to dust thoroughly even where you couldn't see, by hiding sweets, gifts and pennies. She would tell me how many there were around and I would be so proud when I did a good enough job to find them all. Later in life I was lucky enough to coax some of the neighbors to give me some of the recipes that she had shared with them over the years. This is my favorite.

Bobbie Thompson, Class of 1997

Marinara Sauce

1	bell pepper, diced	1	(28 ounce) can peeled tomatoes
2	medium size white onions, diced	8	ounces red table wine
6	cloves garlic, pressed	1	teaspoon salt
1	tablespoon olive oil	1	teaspoon oregano
1	(6 ounce) can tomato paste	3	bay leaves
1	(12 ounce) can tomato sauce	12	ounces beer, optional
		½	teaspoon black pepper
		2	packets sugar substitute

In a large, deep skillet, sauté bell pepper, onion and garlic in olive oil until translucent. At medium heat, add tomato paste, tomato sauce and peeled tomatoes, straining tomatoes through fork to break up. Add all remaining ingredients and simmer slowly, partially covered, for 45 minutes. Reduce to low heat and cook for 30 minutes. Serve over pasta.

Jack Range, Friend of Senior Leaders

Pickled Beets

4	fresh beets	1½	cups white vinegar
2	tablespoons sliced onion	2	tablespoons brown sugar

Cook beets until tender. Reserve juice. Peel off skin and cut. Place beets and onion in a large container and set aside. Bring vinegar, ½ cup reserved juice and sugar to a boil. Heat for 2 minutes. Pour over beets and onions. Chill overnight. Best when marinated over a couple of days.

Ruby Mundy, Class of 1994

"After I retired, I think maybe I was floundering. After you've worked for 40 years you've been focused, but once you retire you find that you're going in a lot of different directions because there are a lot of other people planning your life, too. And you're saying "yes" to everything. And through the LIFE classes, I became empowered. I learned to say NO! I was not going to be running over here and there doing this and that, and I became more focused and decided what I really wanted to do."

Grace Williams, Class of 1996

B. B. Q. Sauce

1½	teaspoons black pepper	4	tablespoons vinegar
1	teaspoon crushed red pepper	4	tablespoons catsup
1	teaspoon granulated sugar	2	tablespoons tomato paste
3	teaspoons salt	2	cloves garlic, chopped
½	teaspoon paprika	2	medium onions, sliced
1½	teaspoons chili powder	2	lemons, sliced
2	teaspoons accent (M.S.G.)	3	bay leaves
1	teaspoon Tabasco sauce	2	sticks butter
1	teaspoon Worcestershire sauce	1	cup oil
		4	cups water

Bring all ingredients to a boil. Lower heat and simmer for 30 minutes.

Jo Nell Dye, Class of 1995

This was my husband's recipe. We used it for many years. Everyone loved his B.B.Q. ribs! He preferred loin ribs. We've had hundreds of cook outs and few left over ribs. About 30 years ago he bought a big, black, cast iron grill from Columbus, GA. He cooked B.B.Q. for the holidays from Spring to Fall. He didn't cook just for the family because it was too much trouble, and the family often had company. He especially liked to cook this for people from out of town who didn't know much about B.B.Q. I would make up potato salad and slaw the day before so that I could relax the day they cooked the meat. The family had a big patio with shade trees, and Bobby could visit and talk while he cooked outside. I recently invited family over for Fourth of July and I made Bobby's sauce; he has passed away. One son came through, smelled it and said "Boy that brings back a ton of memories." And when the oldest son went to cook the ribs he was told, "You have big shoes to fill." I still have his old recipe, all messed up after all of these years. I am going to frame copies of it for all of the children to have in their kitchens.

Squash Relish

½	cup salt	3	tablespoons mustard seed
2	quarts cold water		
2½	quarts chopped butternut squash	12	very small red chili peppers, sliced
1	quart vinegar		Hot chili oil, optional
¾	cup granulated sugar		

Dissolve salt in cold water. Pour over squash and let stand 1 hour. Drain. In a large sauce pan, simmer vinegar, squash and remaining ingredients for 20 minutes. Bring to a boil. Drop 5 drops of chili oil in each sterilized jar before adding ingredients. Immediately pack into jars, leaving ⅛ inch head space. Adjust caps.

Yield: 6 to 7 pints

Dorothy Conyers, Class of 2000

While living in Maine, I had a 12 x 50 foot vegetable garden. I planned my crops so they would yield during our camp meeting at the church in August. One summer I had about 20 butternut squash mature in July and I did not know what to do with them. My son suggested that I make relish and season it with chili oil and peppers. This is the most beautiful relish I have ever made and it is delicious.

Cranberry Orange Relish

4	cups fresh cranberries	1	teaspoon grated orange rind
2	cups granulated sugar		
½	cup water	½	cup slivered almonds
½	cup orange juice		

Combine all ingredients, except almonds, in a sauce pan. Simmer uncovered 10 minutes or until cranberry skins pop, stirring occasionally. Remove from heat and stir in almonds. Cool and store in refrigerator. If desired, serve in lettuce lined orange cups.

Yield: 4 cups

Committee

Some people are born old. Others die at 80 or 90 and don't seem to be old at all. Do you know what I mean?

Zucchini Pickle

22	medium zucchini, sliced	1½	teaspoons turmeric
6	medium onions, sliced	1½	teaspoons mustard seed
⅓	cup salt	1	large bell pepper, cut in
2	ice cube trays of ice		chunks
5	cups granulated sugar	1	(4 ounce) can pimento,
3½	cups white vinegar		drained
1½	teaspoons celery seed	3	garlic cloves, sliced

Place zucchini and onion in a plastic or enamel pan. Sprinkle with salt and add ice cubes. Set overnight. Mix together sugar, vinegar and spices. Bring to boil. Add drained zucchini mixture, bell pepper, pimento and garlic cloves. Simmer for 5 minutes.

Yield: 9 pints

Zeela Porter, Friend of Senior Leaders

One year I had zucchini squash coming out of my ears. I decided to experiment and substitute zucchini for cucumbers for pickling. It worked great.

Blue Cheese Salad Dressing

½	cup mayonnaise	½	cup blue cheese
½	cup dairy sour cream		crumbled
		¼	cup milk

In a blender, combine mayonnaise, sour cream, and ¼ cup blue cheese. Gradually add milk. Remove from blender and add remaining blue cheese. Refrigerate.

Yield: 1¼ cups

Friend of Senior Leaders

Bread and Butter Pickles

4	quarts medium sized cucumbers, unpeeled and sliced	⅓	cup salt
		5	cups granulated sugar
6	medium sized onions, sliced thin	1½	teaspoons turmeric
		1½	teaspoons celery seed
2	green peppers, chopped	2	tablespoons mustard seed
3	whole cloves	3	cups vinegar

Mix first five ingredients thoroughly in covered container with cracked ice. Drain well. In a pot, mix together remaining ingredients. Bring to a boil. Remove from stove. Mix together and seal all ingredients at once in hot sterilized jars.

Yield: approximately 5 quarts

Bridget Ciaramitaro
Executive Director, Senior Leaders

All of my adult life I have thought of myself as older than somebody. Through the LIFE class, I've discovered that retirement gives us the chance to play again and as they say, "Be as young as we feel."

Green Pepper Jelly

¼	cup chopped or ground hot peppers (red or green)	6½	cups granulated sugar
		1½	cups vinegar
		1	bottle liquid pectin
1½	cups chopped sweet green pepper		

Finely grind hot pepper. Mix hot pepper, green pepper, sugar and vinegar in a sauce pan and bring to a boil. Boil for 3 minutes. Add pectin and continue boiling for 1 minute. Remove from heat and let stand for 5 minutes. Pour and seal in sterilized jars. Add green food coloring if desired.

Yield: 7 (½ pint) jars

Jennie Morring, Class of 1993

Sidney's Barbeque Sauce

24	ounces ketchup	3	teaspoons dry mustard
2	cups water	3	teaspoons paprika
1	cup vinegar	3	teaspoons salt
1	cup Worcestershire	3	teaspoons chili powder
	sauce	6	tablespoons plain
1	stick butter		peanut butter
3	teaspoons red pepper		

Simmer together all ingredients for 1 hour. Strain.

Sidney Franklin, J.I.M. Promotions

Soups and Stews

Thanksgiving in Korea — 1951

My husband, Clarence Earl Baugus, Jr., served in the 196th Field Artillery in Korea beginning in September 1950. My children were very small. The youngest was only a little over 4 months old. Those were challenging times for both of us, but we kept in contact by letters. I saved all his letters and in 1980, I began collecting photographs, interviewing other Veterans and documenting the experiences of the 196th Field Artillery.

Clarence Earl was with the Service Battery and he remembered vividly Thanksgiving Day, Thursday, November 22, 1951. The weather was cold, and everyone was homesick. The Army did what it could to make the day festive and bring about some of the warmth that home provides by furnishing turkey and dressing with all the trimmings. Service Battery had a delicious meal consisting of shrimp cocktail, mixed nuts, hard candy, roast turkey, dressing, giblet gravy, creamed potatoes, creamed peas, cranberry sauce, cole slaw, stuffed olives, hot rolls, butter, jelly and coffee. On that day the Battery was about 25 miles north of the 38th parallel at Sohwa-Ri, North Korea.

This meal and the men visiting from other units did lift the spirits, at least for a day. Those were tough times for my husband and me. But we persevered, and needless to say, Savannah, TN was a happy place when Clarence Earl returned home.

Marilyn Baugus, Class of 1992

Rabbit Soup

4	large potatoes	1	parsnip, diced
4	rabbits	4	onions, finely chopped
½	head cabbage, sliced thin	5	carrots, sliced
		⅛	pound butter
1	quart home canned tomatoes	1	tablespoon granulated sugar
2	quarts home canned tomato juice	2	bay leaves
			Herbs to taste
4	turnips, diced		Salt and pepper to taste

Cut potatoes into ¾ inch squares and set aside. Take out buck shots, skin and cut each rabbit into 4 pieces. Place meat into large pot of cold water and boil until meat begins to fall off bone. Remove from broth. Add remaining ingredients to stock. Cook until vegetables are done. Add rabbit and continue to cook until flavor is absorbed.

Mable Harrell, Class of 1993

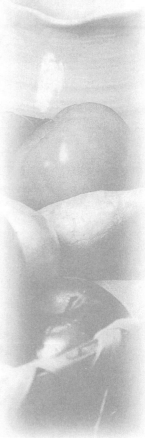

I used to believe that things weren't going to change anyway, so why should I try? I thought getting older was just a downhill course. In LIFE class, I began to believe that I can create my own destiny.

This recipe was prepared in an iron pot dating back to 1805. My grandparents were German and while traveling by wagon in this country they were unable to have their traditional meals. They had to make do with what they could find on the land they traveled, and rabbits were plentiful. After they settled, rabbit soup became a tradition. It was prepared for Christmas Eve each year at the family home of my grandparents. When we went back home each year, this was served after trimming the cedar tree that was cut from the family farm. Everything we ate was grown by my family. Soup was always served with cornbread sticks and corn muffins that were made from corn ground in a grist mill. Even when corn meal was available at local stores, we would still grind our own. For dessert we sat around and ate popcorn while listening to the men tell tales. The children always looked forward to Christmas Eve, warm soup and the tales that were told around the fireplace. To this day the family still gets together in our home town to share rabbit soup and talk around the fireplace. We even have the same big iron pot my grandparents once used for soup.

Seafood and Okra Gumbo

Roux
½ cup all-purpose flour   ½ cup vegetable oil

Holy Trinity
2 cups chopped yellow   ¼ cup vegetable oil
   onions   3 garlic cloves, minced
2 cups chopped scallions   1 teaspoon dried thyme
2 cups chopped bell   1 bay leaf
   pepper   2 teaspoons Cajun
3 large stalks celery,   seasoning
   diced   1 teaspoon salt

Vegetables
1 pound fresh tender okra   1 (28 ounce) can diced
                                   tomatoes

Gumbo   ### Seafood
8 cups homemade   1 pound jumbo crabmeat
   chicken or seafood   1 container fresh oysters
   broth   2 pounds large gulf shrimp

In a cast iron large skillet on low heat, mix together flour and oil until it forms a smooth paste. Stir constantly for approximately 20 minutes. The roux will be a pecan brown color. If it burns, discard and start over. Remove from heat and set aside. In a large cast iron skillet, heat yellow onions, scallions, bell pepper and celery in oil. Sauté and stir, approximately 7 minutes, until tender and yellow onions are transparent. Add remaining Holy Trinity ingredients. Remove from heat and set aside. Add vegetables to Holy Trinity and cook until okra is no longer sticky and ingredients are well blended. In a large heavy pot combine Roux and Holy Trinity mixtures. Slowly add broth, 1 cup at a time, to pot. Turn on heat and bring to gentle boil. Reduce heat to simmer, cover and cook for 2 to 3 hours. Stir occasionally. Gumbo will thicken slightly. One half hour prior to serving gumbo, add crabmeat. Twenty minutes prior to serving, add oysters. Five minutes prior to serving, add shrimp. Shrimp should turn a deep pink color. Serve over cooked long-grain rice in a large soup or gumbo bowl with your favorite hot sauce on the side.

Note: Gumbo can be covered and refrigerated up to 3 days.

Yield: 10 to 12 servings

Sandra Walsh, Friend of Senior Leaders

Seafood and Okra Gumbo *continued*

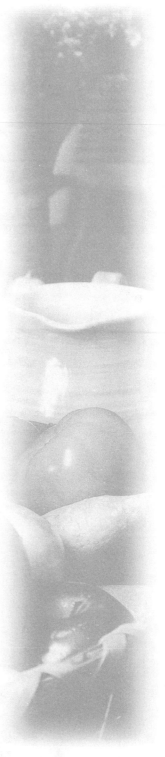

All of the children and grandchildren learn how to make a roux in my family. My parents taught my son, Nathan, at the age of four, who thought that he stirred enough (after three minutes). My mother would then take Nathan to play or read. His papa would then take over and stir, stir and stir until the roux was a beautiful brown. My father died a year ago and we all recall with tears of joy and sadness the many times we cooked gumbo together.

Curry Soup

1	large apple, cored peeled and chopped	1	cup heavy cream
1	large yellow onion, chopped	2	tablespoons curry powder
5	cups chicken stock or canned broth		Salt and pepper to taste

Place apple and onion in a 4 quart pot. Add chicken stock. Bring to a boil, then lower heat and simmer for 20 minutes. Strain into another cooking pot. Add cream in a slow steady stream, stirring with a whisk. Blend in curry powder, salt and pepper. Heat almost to a boil, stirring frequently. Remove from heat. This can be made the night before.

Note: I usually don't strain the apple, onion and broth preferring to have the pulp left in.

Committee

Mock Oyster Soup

1	(16 ounce) can tomatoes	1	quart milk
1	tablespoon baking soda	½	stick butter
			Salt and pepper to taste

Heat tomatoes in a saucepan. Add baking soda. Scoop away foamy layer that forms on top and discard. When tomatoes are clear of foam, add milk, butter, salt and pepper. Heat to boiling, but do not boil. Remove from heat and serve.

Dorothy Conyers, Class of 2000

When I was little, my grandparents used to make this soup and call it Mock Oyster Soup. Growing up in Southeast Missouri, I would not have known an oyster if I had seen one. Nor does the recipe taste like oysters. To this day I don't know why they called it that.

Cajun Shrimp Stew

5	ounces popcorn shrimp, cooked, peeled and de-veined	¼	teaspoon ground black pepper
½	cup chopped celery	1	(16 ounce) can tomatoes
1	medium onion, chopped	8	ounces clams with liquid
1	clove garlic, crushed	14	ounces chicken broth
½	stick butter	¼	teaspoon Tabasco sauce
⅓	cup all-purpose flour	16	ounces okra, cooked and drained
½	teaspoon salt	1	(6 ounce) can crabmeat
½	teaspoon crumbled thyme	3	cups cooked rice
			Chopped walnuts, optional

Rinse and drain shrimp. Set aside. In a soup kettle, sauté celery, onion and garlic in butter until soft. Stir in flour, salt, thyme and pepper stirring constantly until bubbly. Next stir in tomatoes, clams, broth and Tabasco sauce. Stir until thick and boiling. Boil 1 minute. Add shrimp, crabmeat, okra and walnuts. Bring to a boil. Remove from heat and serve over rice in soup bowls.

Rosemary Horton, Class of 1994

Love Soup

LOVE SOUP MIX

1 (16 ounce) package lentils	1 (16 ounce) package tricolored spiral macaroni
1 (16 ounce) package dried peas	1½ cups brown rice
1 (16 ounce) package pearl barley	4 cups dried onions

SOUP

6 cups water	2 (15 ounce) cans tomato sauce
1⅓ cups Love Soup Mix	
3 teaspoons salt	1 (24 ounce) can vegetable juice cocktail
½ teaspoon pepper	
2 carrots, sliced	
2 cups cabbage, shredded	1 pound cooked ground beef, optional

Pour water into a large Dutch oven. Add Love Soup Mix, salt and pepper. Bring to a boil. Add remaining ingredients. Cover and simmer 45 minutes until carrots and cabbage are done.

Yield: 6 to 8 servings

Barbara Gates, Friend of Senior Leaders

This is ideal for gift giving. Put enough Love Mix in a jar for 1 recipe along with the recipe.

The thing I like most about the age I am now is that I am no longer concerned about pleasing other people. I can (and often do) say what needs to be said without thinking of the consequences.

Easy Potato Soup

½ cup Cheddar cheese	1 (15 ounce) can creamed corn
4 medium potatoes, quartered and cooked	1¼ cups milk

Set cheese aside. Blend remaining ingredients. Boil for 3 minutes. Add cheese before serving.

Beverlee Timm, Class of 1994

Margaret Johnson's Good and Easy Soup

2	pounds ground turkey or beef, cooked	¼	head of shredded cabbage
2	large onions, chopped	2	(10 ounce) cans Rotel tomatoes
1	(48 ounce) container V8 Juice	1	(15 ounce) can whole kernel corn
1	(15 ounce) can creamed corn	2	packages dry Italian dressing mix
3	(16 ounce) cans small red beans or black beans		

Combine all ingredients and simmer 2 hours.

Tommie Cervetti, Class of 1994

This soup is so good and so easy. I have a senior friend who always keeps some in the freezer. She says she is not a cook, but she sure cooks this soup.

Sicilian Beans and Greens Soup

A quick and comforting soup.

1	bunch Swiss chard or other mild green	2	(15 ounce) cans white beans, drained and rinsed
2	cloves garlic, chopped	4	(15 ounce) cans water
1	tablespoon oil	1	cup small shell pasta or other small pasta

Wash greens and remove tough parts of stems. Chop leaves and remaining stems into large pieces. In a soup pot, sauté garlic in oil until soft. Add greens and sauté until wilted. Add beans and water. Bring to boil and simmer 20 minutes. Add pasta and cook an additional 20 minutes.

Robert Burns, M.D., Honorary Class of 2000

Salads

*What ever we do to enhance life for ourselves
ultimately improves life for our children,
grandchildren and generations to come.*

Recipe for cooking up love, at home, the way I remember.

3 cups flour	Mixing bowl
¼ pound melted butter	Apron
Egg shells	Bunches of pans
Milk jug	Loose-sleeved shirt
Mixer	Other fun kitchen stuff

First, put your apron on. Tie it loose so it will untie itself when you are halfway through. Push your sleeves up. Put the pans in the oven with nothing in them. Take them out. Use that little brush to slather the butter all over them and make that good cooking smell.

Dump out the flour. Put it in your mixing bowl with that little "holey" thing with a handle. Shake it. Push your sleeves up and say, "Now, I've got flour all over this blouse. I'll have to wash it again."

When all the flour is in the mixing bowl, I think that's when you move the eggs around. They don't go in the bowl, you just sit them on the counter where you are cooking. You might need them later, like you save the newspapers.

Stick the mixer in the bowl and turn it on, knocking against the mixing bowl as much as you can. Stop in mid-mix and say, "Son, will you come tie my apron, my hands are full?" Wait patiently while I figure out how to tie a knot when it's not on my shoe. Say, "Thank you honey. That's fine. Why do I keep using this apron? It won't stay tied."

Put some flour on the countertop and let the dough roll onto it. Get out the rolling pin and smash the dough into a big raw pancake. then ball it up and do it again. Say, "Son will you push these sleeves up please? I've got this stick dough all over my hands." Hold up your hands like Ben Casey and say, "Son, I know I've got flour all over my sleeves, but is not the same as dough. Run along now."

After the bread is finished (how did all that stuff make something so good), call me in for a slice of warm bread and some butter and jelly.

Thanks mom for the memories.

Paul Renfroe, Class of 1997

Fresh Strawberry Toss

DRESSING
½ teaspoon salt
½ teaspoon pepper
2 tablespoons granulated sugar
2 tablespoons vinegar
¼ cup vegetable oil
1 tablespoon chopped parsley
Dash red pepper sauce

TOPPING
¼ cup sliced almonds
1 tablespoon plus 1 teaspoon granulated sugar

SALAD
¼ head iceberg lettuce
¼ head romaine lettuce
1 cup chopped celery
2 green onions, thinly sliced
12 fresh strawberries, halved

Combine all dressing ingredients in a tightly covered jar, shake and refrigerate. In a skillet, sprinkle almonds with sugar and cook over low heat. Stir constantly until sugar is melted and almonds are coated. Cool on aluminum foil and break apart. Store at room temperature. Rinse and dry lettuce. Tear into bite-size pieces. Place lettuce, celery and onions in a plastic refrigerator storage bag. Secure bag and refrigerate up to 24 hours. About 5 minutes before serving, pour dressing into bag, add strawberries and shake until onions and strawberries are well-coated. Sprinkle almonds over salad and serve.

Yield: 4 to 6 servings

Mary Jo Williams, Friend of Senior Leaders

I was at a wedding once. My husband was officiating. We were close friends of the couple getting married. We were all standing at the altar and I was crying. My husband took the communion cloth and gave it me to wipe the tears. That is a gesture of love, a memory that I hope no matter how old I get, I will not forget.

Bridget Ciaramitaro

Baked Chicken Salad

2	cups cooked chicken, cut up	½	teaspoon salt
1	cup cream of chicken soup	1	tablespoon lemon juice
		¾	cup mayonnaise
2	teaspoons minced onion	¼	teaspoon pepper
½	cup chopped pecans	3	hard-boiled eggs, chopped
1	cup diced celery	1	cup crushed crackers

Mix all ingredients except crackers. Put in greased baking dish. Top with crackers. Bake at 350 degrees for 25 minutes.

Yield: 4 to 6 servings

Nelly Galloway Shearer, Friend of Senior Leaders

This recipe is from a Virginia Tech Cookbook while visiting the campus in the 1970s. It is an easy "make ahead" recipe which can be prepared ahead and refrigerated. However, don't add crackers until just before serving. Potato chips are also good on top.

Hot Seafood Salad

1	large green pepper, chopped	1	teaspoon Worcestershire sauce
1	small onion, chopped	½	teaspoon salt
1	cup diced celery		Dash of pepper
¾	cup flaked crabmeat	1	cup bread crumbs
½	cup shrimp, cut up	½	stick butter
1	cup oysters		Paprika, optional
1	cup mayonnaise		

Mix together all ingredients except bread crumbs, butter and paprika. Place in casserole dish. Top with bread crumbs and lightly drizzle butter. Bake at 350 degrees for 45 minutes. Sprinkle with paprika if desired. Serve hot.

Yield: 4 servings

Jennie Morring, Class of 1993

Dorothy's Spaghetti Salad

1 (16 ounce) bag thin
   spaghetti
1 red onion, chopped
1 green pepper, chopped
1 tomato, chopped

10 ounces chopped ham
1 (16 ounce) bottle Italian
   dressing
¼ container McCormick's
   Salad Supreme

Cook spaghetti noodles, drain and cool. In a large bowl, mix together onion, green pepper, tomato and ham. Add ½ of Italian dressing. Stir with spoon until well blended. Add more dressing, continuing to mix until thoroughly covered. Garnish salad with Salad Supreme. Refrigerate. Best when prepared overnight.

Note: Other vegetables can be added to this recipe.

Dorothy Adams, Class of 1999

Before retiring, I was employed at Bell South Telephone Company. We used to celebrate many special occasions with potluck luncheons. This became one of my favorite dishes because it is so delicious, low in calories and easy to make. I hope you enjoy it as much as my co-workers, family and friends have for many years.

Hot Chicken Salad

3   cups boiled chicken, diced
¾   cup uncooked rice
1   cup mayonnaise
1   (10¾ ounce) can cream of chicken soup
1   (10¾ ounce) can cream of celery soup

1   (4½ ounce) can water chestnuts, sliced
1   (2 ounce) jar pimento, diced
1½ cups green beans, drained
1   medium onion, diced

TOPPING

1½ sticks butter, melted
2   cups grated Cheddar cheese

2   cups fine bread crumbs

Season chicken as desired. Set aside. Boil rice in reserved chicken broth. In a large bowl mix together chicken, rice, mayonnaise, soups, chestnuts, pimento, beans and onion. Place in 3 quart casserole dish. Combine butter, cheese and bread crumbs. Spread over salad. Bake at 350 degrees for 45 minutes or until bubbly.

Note: Broccoli may be used in place of green beans. This dish freezes well.

Evelyn Cornelius, Class of 1993

Low Fat Sugar Free Fruit Salad

1   pint fat free cottage cheese
20 ounces crushed pineapple, drained
2   (3 ounce) packages sugar free orange jello

12½ ounces Mandarin oranges, drained
1   (3 ounce) jar maraschino cherries, drained
8   ounces light Cool Whip

Mix together ingredients and chill for 24 hours. Stir and serve.

Teresa Lewis, Class of 1997

Baja Chicken-Pasta Salad

1 cup uncooked orzo or ring macaroni	½ cup mayonnaise or salad dressing
1 (6 ounce) package diced dried mixed fruit	2 tablespoons plain yogurt or sour cream
2 cups cut-up cooked chicken	1 teaspoon ground red chiles
1 cup cubed jícama	¼ teaspoon salt
2 green onions, sliced	

Cook orzo as directed on package. While cooking, stir in fruit. Rinse orzo and fruit with cold water. Drain and set aside. Mix chicken, orzo, fruit, jícama and onions. In a separate bowl, combine remaining ingredients. Toss into chicken mixture. Cover and chill for at least 2 hours.

Yield: 6 servings

Lawyer Cummings, Class of 1997

Pineapple Party Salad

1 (3 ounce) package pistachio pudding	20 ounces Cool Whip Maraschino cherries, optional
2 pounds cottage cheese	Pecans, optional
1 (8 ounce) can crushed pineapple, drained	

In a large bowl, sprinkle pistachio pudding over cottage cheese and mix well. Stir in drained pineapple. Fold in 12 ounces Cool Whip. Spread remaining Cool Whip on top. Decorate with maraschino or pecans. Refrigerate.

Helen Lockhart, Class of 1995

Beauty, beauty, beauty. We are so focused on a connection between youth and beauty or good looks and beauty when it comes to people. Yet wine improves with age, antiques are more valued than new pieces, a tree is more beautiful at 100 than it was as a seedling. There is beauty in aging. I've seen it in hundreds of faces even my own.

Apricot Salad

16	ounces crushed pineapple	2	cups buttermilk
6	ounces apricot jello, prepared	8	ounces Cool Whip

Combine pineapple and jello. Heat to a boil, then let it cool. Add buttermilk and Cool Whip. Chill over night.

Louise Brown, Class of 1994

Heavenly Salad

2	tablespoons granulated sugar	1	cup pineapple juice
1	(3 ounce) package lime jello	1	(8 ounce) can crushed pineapple, drained
1	cup boiling water Green food coloring, optional	1	(4 ounce) bottle maraschino cherries, drained and chopped
1½	(3 ounce) packages cream cheese	½	cup chopped walnuts
		1	cup whipping cream, whipped

Mix together sugar and jello. Dissolve in boiling water. Add food coloring as desired. Whip cream cheese in a mixer with ½ of pineapple juice. Add cream cheese mixture and remaining juice to hot jello mixture. Stir until cream cheese is melted. Chill until set. Add pineapple, cherries and walnuts to jello mixture. Gently fold in whipped cream. Pour into pan mold or flat dish. Chill until firm. Unmold or cut in squares to serve.

Yield: 8 to 10 servings

Note: To reduce calories you may substitute sugar-free jello for regular jello, Neufchâtel cheese for cream cheese, and 1 packet dream whip for whipped cream.

Lorraine Kauffman, Class of 1992

Dream Salad

1 (8 ounce) container sour cream or Cool Whip	1½ cups Mandarin oranges, drained
1 (16 ounce) bag colored marshmallows	1 (3½ ounce) can coconut
	1 (8 ounce) can pineapple chunks, drained

Mix sour cream and marshmallows. Add remaining ingredients. Chill 3 hours and serve.

Jacqueline Randolph, Class of 1992

This recipe has been in my family for many years. It is always served for Easter Sunday dinner or any other time of year we want a light and refreshing salad.

Apple-Raspberry Salad

1 (3 ounce) package raspberry gelatin	1 cup applesauce
1 cup boiling water	1 cup sour cream
1 (10 ounce) package frozen raspberries	1 cup tiny marshmallows

Dissolve gelatin in boiling water. Add frozen raspberries and stir until thawed. Once gelatin has dissolved add applesauce. Pour into 6 x 10 inch dish. Chill until set. Combine sour cream and marshmallows. Spread over gelatin mixture. Cover and chill for 1 to 2 hours. Serve on lettuce leaf.

Evelyn Cornelius, Class of 1993

"Because of the LIFE classes, I am now able to communicate my feelings, thoughts and opinions to my family, doctors and others. They always made decisions for me. I needed to make up my own mind, say "no" when I needed to. I felt a lot of growth. I now determine my own direction.

Geneva Burns, Class of 1996

Pretzel Salad

LAYER ONE

1½ stick butter
3   tablespoons granulated
     sugar

2¼ cups crushed pretzels

LAYER TWO

1   cup granulated sugar
1   (8 ounce) package
     cream cheese

1   (8 ounce) container
     Cool Whip

LAYER THREE

2   (3 ounce) packages
     strawberry jello
2   cups boiling water

1   (16 ounce) bag frozen
     strawberries

Cream butter and sugar. Add pretzels and press into 9 x 12 inch oven proof dish. Bake at 350 degrees for 10 minutes. Let cool. Cream sugar and cream cheese. Add cool whip and spread over cooled pretzel layer. Mix jello and boiling water until dissolved. Add strawberries. Let partially jell and pour over second layer. Refrigerate overnight.

Mal Shapiro, Class of 1994

This salad was served by the ladies at First Presbyterian Church in Holly Springs, Mississippi during the Holly Springs Pilgrimage. The many delicious dishes served by the church ladies made this a most enjoyable day.

Joy is the magic of movies old and new.

Avocado Aspic

1	package lemon jello	1	tablespoon vinegar
1½	cups hot water	1	tablespoon
2	cups avocado pulp		Worcestershire sauce
½	teaspoon scraped onion	½	teaspoon salt

Dissolve jello in hot water. Chill. Press avocado through sieve for pulp. Mix remaining ingredients and fold into first mixture. When it begins to set, turn it into a shallow dish approximately 8 x 12 inches that has been rinsed with cold water. Chill until firm. Cut in portions and serve on lettuce. Garnish with tomato wedge, hard boiled egg and mayonnaise.

Lou Jamison, Class of 1992

Tabbouleh
(Cracked Wheat Salad)

1	cup cracked wheat	1	green pepper, chopped
¾	cup lemon juice	1	cucumber, peeled and
2	bunches chopped		chopped
	parsley leaves	2	large tomatoes,
1	teaspoon dried mint		chopped
1	teaspoon paprika	1	tablespoon salt
2	garlic cloves, minced		Lemon juice to taste
1	green onion, chopped	1	cup olive oil

Place cracked wheat in bowl. Add lemon juice, parsley, mint, paprika and garlic. Mix in vegetables. Add salt and lemon. Add olive oil. Chill for 1 hour. Serve with romaine lettuce or pita bread wedges.

Yield: 12 servings

Shoghig (Sunny) Ross, Senior Leaders Board of Directors

Potato Salad

	Potatoes, cubed and cooked	2	teaspoons mustard
4	eggs, boiled	1	teaspoon salt
2	cups milk		Pepper to taste
½	cup vinegar		Mayonnaise

Cook and cube potatoes. Chop boiled eggs. Set aside. Combine remaining ingredients and bring to boil, stirring constantly. Pour heated sauce over potatoes. Toss in eggs. Chill. Serve cold.

Marilyn Wilson, Friend of Senior Leaders

This recipe came from my Dad's side of the family. When I asked Mom if it was a German recipe handed down, all she could tell me was she got it from my Aunt Leon. Dad's mom died when my parents had only been married a couple of years. Mom was 19 when she married. This is the only potato salad my husband will eat, and he also likes it hot from the stove. It doesn't last long at my house. I have passed this recipe on to my youngest daughter. It is now her favorite and anytime we have a barbeque to cookout, she calls and tells me I must make my potato salad. Then she takes most of it home to have for lunch at work.

Broccoli Salad

SALAD

1	bunch broccoli	8	slices crisp bacon, crumbled
½	cup raisins		
½	cup chopped onion		

DRESSING

2	tablespoons granulated sugar	2	tablespoons vinegar
		1	cup mayonnaise

Chop broccoli heads into bite size pieces. Add raisins and onion. Stir. In a small bowl, mix together sugar, vinegar and mayonnaise. Pour dressing over broccoli mixture and marinate in refrigerator. Before serving top with bacon.

Committee

Mashed Potato Salad

4-5	medium potatoes, peeled and quartered	2	tablespoons vinegar
¼	cup milk	½	cup salad dressing (not mayonnaise)
½	cup butter Additional seasoning, optional	3	hard-boiled eggs, chopped
¼	cup minced onion	1	tablespoon prepared mustard
¼	cup minced sweet pickles		Salt and pepper to taste

Peel and quarter 4 to 5 medium potatoes. Boil potatoes until tender and mash in a large bowl. Blend in milk, butter and seasoning. Add to the potato mixture minced onion, sweet pickles, vinegar and salad dressing. Fold in ⅔ of chopped eggs. Stir in prepared mustard. Add salt and pepper to taste. Garnish with remaining ⅓ of chopped eggs. This is a wonderful dish served either hot or cold.

Nelda Grimes, Class of 1992

Festive Wagon Wheel Pasta Salad

1	pound wagon wheel pasta, cooked	½	cup diced red sweet pepper
½	pound Cheddar cheese, cubed	1	cup coarsely chopped sweet pickles
1½	cups finely diced celery	½	cup grated red onion French dressing

Combine all ingredients, using enough French dressing to moisten as desired. Refrigerate at least overnight. Stir occasionally to distribute dressing over ingredients.

Grace Williams, Class of 1996

English Pea Salad

½	cup sour cream
½	cup mayonnaise or Cool Whip
1	(16 ounce) package frozen peas

Spanish peanuts
Crisp crumbled bacon, optional

Combine sour cream and mayonnaise. Add frozen peas and peanuts. Top with crisp crumbled bacon.

Beverlee Timm, Class of 1994

Rodeo Salad

1	package macaroni and cheese dinner
2	cups kidney beans, drained

¼ cup sliced green onion
⅓ cup sliced sweet pickle
½ cup Miracle Whip salad dressing

Prepare dinner as directed. Add remaining ingredients. Toss lightly. Chill.

Yield: 4 to 6 servings

Louise Fowler, Friend of Senior Leaders

Kidney Bean Salad

3	cups cooked kidney beans, drained
½	cup chopped sweet pickles

5 hard-boiled eggs, chopped
¾ cup diced celery
1 cup mayonnaise

Combine beans, pickles, eggs and celery. Toss lightly. Add mayonnaise and blend. Chill.

Yield: 4 to 6 servings

Jennie Morring, Class of 1993

Breads

Joy is a little voice on the telephone,
"Hi Grandma!"

Vic's Sweet Bread

5	cups all-purpose flour	4	tablespoon granulated sugar
1	teaspoon salt	2	tablespoons dry milk
1½	cups hot water	3	tablespoons oil
2	teaspoons dry yeast		

In a large bowl, mix together flour and salt. Make a well in center of flour mixture. Into well, put, in order, water, dry yeast, sugar, milk and oil. Mix with mixer or large spoon. Use (clean!) hands to mix bread to a satiny finish. If too dry or not satiny, add milk a little at a time. If sticky, add flour a little at a time to get it satiny. Knead dough until it does not stick to hands, about 5 minutes. Cover bowl and put in a place away from cool air. I put mine in the microwave. Allow dough to double in bulk. Cut dough in half. Place into 2 greased bread pans and allow to rise and double in size. Heat oven to 400 degrees. Place bread in oven and bake for 20 minutes or until golden brown. Remove from pans immediately to a wire rack.

Victor Como, LIFE Class of 2000

This came from my mother's recipe of bread making. There are so many things I could write about bread, so I just thought I would share some feelings that are close to my heart. When I make bread, I feel close to God. The enjoyment of baking bread gives me deeply felt emotional satisfaction. All my family, 13 brothers and sisters, as well as my children and grandchildren, have all felt this way. My mother, father and grandparents led the way to our love of breadmaking. Years ago, when the world was more rural, nearly any child knew the basic recipe for bread - flour, yeast, salt and water - in different proportions. Bread started by being baked in the sun, under a pile of hot ashes, on a baking stone or on a griddle. Often it was rather hard, dry and gritty. Even as it was, it probably was, and still is, a treat when you ate it while it was still hot. Even now it is a pleasure to feel the dough in my hands as I make bread from scratch. People, like me and many others, are fearful of the future and skeptical of technological advances in food preparation because our strong heart felt feelings for the past connect us with the smells, sights and sounds of home and family.

Ice Box Rolls

2	packages active dry yeast	1	cup mashed Irish potatoes
½	cup warm water	1	cup milk
½	cup vegetable oil	2	eggs, beaten
½	cup granulated sugar		All-purpose flour
1	teaspoon salt		

Lightly oil the inside of a large bowl and set aside. In another bowl, pour yeast into warm water to dissolve. Combine all ingredients. Turn mix on a smooth flat surface working in flour until dough forms a soft ball. Place dough into the oiled bowl. Flip bottom side up to grease both sides. Cover and let stand in a warm place for about 1 hour. The dough should double in size. Refrigerate over night and roll out onto a floured surface. Cut like biscuits and place on a greased baking sheet. Let rise again for at least 1 hour until the dough doubles in size. Bake at 350 degrees for 20 minutes or until brown.

Note: I butter the top with a pastry brush when almost brown. Originally, these rolls were made in a large wooden dough bowl and mixed by hand like biscuits.

Novella Schulte, Class of 1995

Do you know where Potneck is? Well few people do or will admit they do. It is a place where Stewart County's northwest corner meets Kentucky at a bend in the Cumberland. Reportedly this was the home of the best "corn liker" ever made. I don't know - I don't remember ever having tasted any. The greater part of my childhood was spent here. This recipe was given to me some time in those years, notice the title, "Ice Box Rolls." We actually had an ice box back then. We didn't have a refrigerator until TVA came to Tennessee. I have always enjoyed making bread. Try it! It's good!

Yeast Rolls

1	cup shortening	2	eggs, beaten
5½	cups all-purpose flour	1	cup boiling water
1	cup granulated sugar	2	packages quick rise yeast
1	teaspoon salt	1	cup warm water

Preheat oven to 350 degrees. Mix shortening, flour, sugar, salt, eggs and boiling water. In a small bowl, mix together yeast with warm water. Add to flour mixture. Cover bowl with towel and let set 5 to 6 hours. Barely knead dough, pinch and put into muffin tins. Bake for 15 to 20 minutes.

Yield: 3 dozen

Lillie Nelson, Class of 1992

This recipe was always doubled at our house and made in two batches. Rolls were a treat, and we loved them hot or cold. Is it just me who thinks the smells are different now than when we were young? — Oh happy day, the smell still lingers as we come home from church on Sunday.

Monkey Bread

1	(10 count) can biscuits	½	cup brown sugar
⅓	cup granulated sugar	¼	cup chopped pecans,
2	teaspoons cinnamon		optional
½	cup margarine		

Cut biscuits into quarters. Mix sugar and cinnamon in a bag. Place quartered biscuits in bag and shake to coat. Place coated biscuits into ungreased round cake pan. Melt margarine with brown sugar and pour on biscuits. Sprinkle on pecans if desired. Bake at 400 degrees for 20 minutes.

Waldine Robinson, Class of 1995

I started a journal in LIFE class. What a stress reducer! And best of all I have discovered that inside me there are many wisdoms to share. I hope that someday, my grandchildren will read my journal and know of the many opportunities that lie ahead.

Graduate, Class of 1995

When my father died, my brother had regrets. "There is more I wanted to say." I had no regrets. I had been blessed to have said it all.

Cinnamon Yeast Rolls

ROLLS

6	cups all-purpose flour	2	packages dry yeast
2	eggs	1	cup of hot water
1	stick butter	1	cup warm water
4	tablespoons granulated sugar		

FILLING

1	cup firmly packed brown sugar	½	cup raisins
1	teaspoon cinnamon	1	(16 ounce) can crushed pineapple, cooked until juice is low

GLAZE

1	cup powdered sugar	½	cup water

Combine all ingredients for rolls and let sit. Roll out dough very thin and butter top. Spread brown sugar, cinnamon, raisins and cooked pineapple over the top of dough. Roll up and place in a pan. Butter the top and let rise. Cook at 350 degrees for 30 minutes or until brown. Remove from oven and lightly glaze.

Lucille Jackson, Class of 1995

"LIFE classes have given me the opportunity to reach other people that maybe would not otherwise have gotten the information. We must share what we have learned with others."

Audrey Larsha, Class of 1997

My aunt, who used to be a cook in Mississippi, taught me how to make plain rolls while I was in the Corinth, MS Elementary School. Over the years, I did this first by adding cinnamon, butter and sugar, then raisins and pineapple. I am retired now and sometimes get bored. When this happens, I go to the kitchen to pass the time. I cook this recipe often and share it with friends and family.

Biscuits

Biscuits were the first thing my mother taught me to cook. This is a great example of how many people learned to cook in the old days. Most didn't even own measuring cups and spoons. They learned by watching others and by trial and error.

half a large bowl .... all-purpose flour
few smidgens .... baking powder
3-4 pinches .... baking soda
several dashes .... salt
big glob .... shortening
enough to moisten .... buttermilk

Preheat oven to 375 degrees. Grease 2 baking pans and set aside. Fill a large bowl half full of flour. Add baking powder, baking soda, salt and mix well. Cut in shortening. Pour in buttermilk until moistened. If dough becomes too thick, add a tad more buttermilk. If dough becomes too thin, add a dab of flour. Knead dough on a dough board until you think your arms will fall off. Roll smooth with a rolling pin. Cut out biscuits with a tin can with the top cut out and holes punched in the bottom. Bake until light brown. Serve hot. If you happen to drop one on the floor don't put it back on the platter; kick it under the table - the dog'll eat it. It won't hurt none to ask the Lord to bless them.

Bertha Brasfield, Class of 1995

I was 10 years old when my mother taught me to cook biscuits, the first thing I ever learned to cook. I grew up out in the country, the 2nd of 9 children. We worked hard and were not fussy about what we ate back then. My family's routine was to get up and eat a large, filling breakfast to tide us over in the fields until we returned for a noon day meal. Since food was cooked on a wood stove, the heat was intense, so my mother would often make up a lot of corn bread early in the day while it was still cool so as not to have a fire at noontime. My sister and I would sometimes find where our mother had hidden the cornbread, and so the family wouldn't have enough for the noon or evening meal.

Big Mama's Biscuits

2 cups all-purpose flour	½ teaspoon granulated
½ teaspoon salt	sugar
2½ teaspoons baking	½ cup shortening
powder	½ cup milk
	½ cup soft butter

In a mixing bowl, sift flour, baking powder and salt. Cut in shortening until dough forms small beads. Add milk gradually and knead lightly until smooth ball is formed. On lightly floured board, roll out dough to ½ inch thickness. Cut with biscuit cutter or glass. Spread butter on top of each biscuit before baking. Bake at 450 degrees for about 10 minutes. Serve with molasses and butter, Honey Butter, jelly or preserves.

Esther "Lo" Dawson, Friend of Senior Leaders

Smiles are so contagious. Try smiling or even laughing in the doctor's waiting room.

Big Mama, Sadie Smith, is 99 years old. Although she doesn't cook anymore, she clearly remembered this recipe. She is a remarkable "young" woman. When I was a little girl, coming home from school was the greatest because I was going to Big Mama's house. Everyday Big Mama would have a treat ready for me. I would quickly go in, take off my coat and head for the table. She would bring a plate of hot, fresh homemade biscuits with Delta molasses or Karo syrup, and sit them right in front of me. I, without hesitation, would devour every one, morsel by morsel. It was always fun to play in the thick stringy molasses that drips from the biscuit onto my chin or shirt as I ate. With a full tummy I would say, "Big Mama that was sooo good! Thank you!" She'd laugh, "You love my biscuits. Did you get enough?" I couldn't eat anymore if I wanted to I thought as I sopped the last few crumbs in the molasses. Then after putting my dishes away, I would do my homework or play outside and wait until the next day to savor her soft, chewy biscuits that she seemed to make especially for me.

Whole Wheat Biscuits

1	cup all-purpose flour	1	teaspoon salt
1	cup wheat flour	¾	cup skim milk
1	tablespoon baking powder	⅛	cup apple sauce
		⅛	cup canola oil

Mix together dry ingredients. Add remaining ingredients. Mix well until dough forms a sticky ball. Place dough onto a floured cutting board. Knead dough lightly flouring surface regularly to avoid sticking. Knead until dough contracts and is soft. Flatten to ½ inch and cut with a biscuit cutter or top of drinking glass. Bake at 400 degrees for 10 minutes.

Heather Baugus, Honorary Class of 1998

I find that the process of baking is a very calming activity. It is almost an art form in and of itself. The final product is just "icing on the cake". And what is more delicious than bread hot out of the oven? What I love most about this recipe is that it's simple and nutritious. Who says you can't have a great breakfast on the run?

Strawberry Swirl

⅔ cup shortening
⅔ cup granulated sugar
2 cups all-purpose flour
2 teaspoons baking powder
½ teaspoon salt
½ teaspoon baking soda
½ teaspoon ground nutmeg
2 eggs, beaten
⅔ cup buttermilk
½ cup strawberry preserves
¼ cup chopped walnuts

Cream shortening and sugar. In a separate bowl, mix together flour, baking powder, salt, baking soda and nutmeg. Add to creamed mixture. Mix well. Reserve ½ cup for topping. Combine eggs and buttermilk. Add to remaining flour mixture, stirring just until blended. Spread into greased 9 x 9 x 2 inch baking pan. Drop preserves in spoonfuls on top of batter. Swirl through batter with spatula to marble. Stir nuts into reserved crumb mixture. Sprinkle on top. Bake at 375 degrees for 30 minutes.

Yield: 8 to 9 servings

Heather Baugus, Honorary Class of 1998

"One of the things that I gained from LIFE class is that it caused me to have an awareness that, regardless of ethnic, cultural or social background, we all have wants and needs and that we have been empowered to work on and address these things."

*Bobbie Thompson,
Class of 1997*

When I was growing up, no matter what time of year it was, my mother, father and brother always looked forward to Christmas. It was the most celebrated holiday for us. Of course, we all looked forward to different things. My mother and father would spend all year searching for that one special ornament to add to the tree. They would also spend endless hours trying to find the "perfect gift" for my brother and me, those gifts that would cause any little kid's eyes and mouth to open wide. My brother and I, of course, looked forward to what most kids would, Christmas presents. As we grew older, we began instead to look forward to the time spent with family, the tradition of putting up the tree (now four trees), and awakening at my parents' house on Christmas morning. It is harder now to be together for all of these precious moments. But I will never forget them. Over the past several years, this special Christmas treat has become symbolic of the many Christmas mornings I have shared with them. It is the holiday recipe that I cherish most.

Plum Coffee Cake

CAKE

2	cups granulated sugar	2	cups all-purpose flour
1	cup oil	½	teaspoon salt
3	eggs	½	teaspoon baking soda
2	teaspoons red food coloring	1	teaspoon cinnamon
		1	teaspoon ground clove
2	small jars plum baby food	1	cup chopped nuts

GLAZE

2½	tablespoons lemon juice	1	teaspoon red food coloring
¼	cup butter		
1	cup confectioners' sugar		

Beat sugar, oil and eggs. Blend in food coloring and plums. Add remaining ingredients. Mix well. Pour into greased and floured Bundt pan. Bake at 325 degrees for 60 to 70 minutes or until done. Cool in pan 5 minutes. Remove from pan. For glaze, combine lemon juice, butter, sugar and food coloring in a saucepan. Heat until butter is melted. Remove from heat and stir until smooth. Brush hot cake with ½ glaze. Let stand 20 minutes. Brush with remaining glaze.

Victoria Smith, Class of 1994

Key Lime Bread

Bread

¾	cup butter, melted	3	cups all-purpose flour
2	cups granulated sugar	2	teaspoons baking
4	eggs		powder
½	teaspoon vanilla	1	cup milk
2	lime rinds, grated	1	cup chopped nuts
½	teaspoon salt		

Glaze

2	limes, juiced	½	cup confectioners' sugar

Blend butter and sugar together. Add eggs one at a time, beating well after each addition. Stir in vanilla and grated lime rinds. Combine flour and baking powder. Add alternately with milk into batter. Mix well. Fold in nuts. Pour into 2 greased 9 x 5 inch loaf pans. Bake at 350 degrees for 50 minutes or until done. While baking, combine glaze ingredients. Spoon glaze over hot bread in pans. Cool 10 minutes and remove from pans. Best sliced and served the next day.

Lou Jamison, Class of 1992

Streusel Filled Coffee Cake

> "What I enjoy most in life is watching my grandchildren."
>
> *Graduate,*
> *Class of 1999*

CAKE

1½	cups all-purpose flour	¼	cup butter, softened
¾	cup granulated sugar	1	egg, beaten
1	tablespoon baking powder	½	cup milk
		1	teaspoon vanilla
¼	teaspoon salt		

STREUSEL

½	cup brown sugar	2	tablespoons melted butter
2	tablespoons flour		
2	teaspoons cinnamon	½	cup pecan pieces

Sift together flour, sugar, baking powder and salt. Cut in butter until mixture resembles coarse meal. In a separate bowl, mix together egg, milk and vanilla. Add to dry ingredients. Mix just to dampen. For streusel, mix together sugar, flour and cinnamon with fork. Stir in butter and nuts. Spread ½ of batter in an 8 inch pan. Sprinkle ½ of streusel over batter. Repeat. Bake at 375 degrees for 30 minutes.

Georgia Bartosch, Class of 1992

My sister would bake this quick coffee cake a day before she knew we would be driving up from Memphis to spend the week end with her in St. Louis. Our family was transferred to Memphis in 1972, and we have been very happy down here.

Sausage Mini Muffins

1	pound "hot" sausage, cooked and drained	1	(11⅛ ounces) can nacho cheese soup
½	cup grated sharp Cheddar cheese	⅔	cup water
		3	cups biscuit baking mix

In a large bowl, mix together sausage, cheese, soup and water. Stir in biscuit baking mix 1 cup at a time. Pour into greased mini-muffin pan and bake at 350 degrees for 10 to 12 minutes.

Note: These are easy to prepare and great with meals or as a snack.

Yeild: 2 dozen

Jean Webb, Class of 1993

Bran Muffins

½ cup Bran Buds
4½ tablespoons shortening
    or margarine
½ cup boiling water
¾ cup granulated sugar
1¼ cups all-purpose flour
1¼ teaspoons soda
¼ teaspoon salt

1 egg, beaten
1 cup buttermilk
1¼ cups All Bran cereal
¼ cup seeded Muscat
    raisins or chopped
    dates
Chopped nuts, optional

Pour boiling water over bran buds and shortening. Mix until shortening is melted. Add sugar and blend. Sift together dry ingredients and add to sugar mixture. Add remaining ingredients. Mix thoroughly. Pour into greased muffin pan ¾ full. Bake at 400 degrees for 15 minutes. This makes a light, tender and moist muffin.

Note: If you are unable to find Bran Buds, additional All Bran can be used. If using dates, soften in hot water and drain. Batter will keep in the refrigerator, covered, for up to six weeks.

Mrs. Frances Crain, Friend of Senior Leaders

This is my most requested recipe. During the 1960s, I was working in Chicago and living alone in an apartment. I traveled about a third of the time and returning from one trip I stopped by for a visit with my brother and his family. My sister-in-law baked some of these muffins. I fell in love with them and asked for the recipe. For the past twenty years, I have had Sunday morning neighborhood breakfasts. The breakfast everyone loves the most consists of sausage, fried apples and these muffins.

Oatmeal Bran Muffins

1½	cups oat bran	⅓	cup honey
¾	cup old-fashioned rolled oats	2	tablespoons safflower oil
½	teaspoon salt	¾	cup skim milk
½	teaspoon nutmeg	1	(4 ounce) carton egg substitute
1	teaspoon cinnamon		
2	teaspoons baking powder	1	teaspoon vanilla
½	cup brown sugar	¼	cup raisins, soaked in hot water

Preheat oven to 425 degrees. Mix together dry ingredients. In a separate bowl, mix together remaining ingredients. Add to dry ingredients. Mix well. Fill greased muffin tins ⅔ full. Bake for 15 to 17 minutes.

Note: You can substitute chopped nuts or blueberries for raisins if preferred.

Yield: 1 dozen

Helen Lockhart, Class of 1995

Veggie Corn Muffin Mix

1	package corn muffin mix	⅓	cup milk
		1	cup grated carrots
1	egg	1	cup chopped broccoli

Preheat oven to 400 degrees. Grease muffin pans or line with paper baking cups. Blend all ingredients. Batter will be slightly lumpy. Fill cups full with batter. Bake for 15 to 20 minutes or until golden brown.

Note: For maximum crown on muffins, let batter rest for 3 to 4 minutes before filling cups.

Joyce Killebrew, Friend of Senior Leaders

This recipe is a fun way to get children to eat their vegetables.

Pumpkin Muffins

1	cup cooked, drained and mashed pumpkin	1	egg, beaten
¾	cup brown sugar	1¾	cups all-purpose flour
¼	cup molasses	1	teaspoon baking soda
½	cup butter, softened	¼	teaspoon salt
		¼	cup pecans, optional

I use to think happy people were those who only had good things happen to them. Boy, was I wrong. Happy people learn to deal with life's traumas and move on.

Strain pumpkin. Cream sugar, molasses and butter. Add egg and pumpkin. Blend well. In a separate bowl, mix flour with soda and salt. Beat into pumpkin batter. Fold in pecans. Pour batter into greased muffin pans ½ full. Bake at 375 degrees for 20 minutes.

Note: To reduce fat and cholesterol, substitute low calorie margarine for butter, 2 egg whites for 1 egg, walnuts for pecans and reduce brown sugar to ½ cup.

Bridget Ciaramitaro, Executive Director of Senior Leaders

When we started LIFE classes in 1992, we had no idea what a success they would be. It wasn't long after the first graduation, that graduates of the program began gathering around my dining room table to plan for the future of an organization that would be led by seniors. These pumpkin muffins were served at many of these meetings.

Butter Muffins

2	cups self-rising flour	1	cup butter, melted
1	(8 ounce) container sour cream		

Stir together all ingredients just until blended. Spoon into lightly greased mini-muffin pans, filling to top. Bake at 350 degrees for 25 minutes or until lightly browned.

Yield: 2½ dozen

Patria Johnson, Friend of Senior Leaders

Cracklin' Corn Bread

1	cup plain cornmeal	¼	teaspoon baking soda
2	heaping tablespoons all-purpose flour	1	cup buttermilk
1	tablespoon baking powder	1	egg
		2	tablespoons bacon drippings
½	teaspoon salt	½	cup pork cracklins

Preheat oven to 400 degrees. Mix together cornmeal, flour, baking powder, salt and baking soda. Add buttermilk and egg, mixing well. Heat bacon drippings in an iron skillet. Pour off most of grease into batter and mix. Stir cracklins into mixture. Pour batter into hot skillet and place in center of oven. Bake until top looks dry and cracked. Turn oven to broil and brown top. Turn out onto a plate and serve.

Marilyn Baugus, Class of 1992

This is one of the first things I learned to cook as a young girl. This makes great cornbread if you just leave out the cracklins.

Mexican Corn Bread

1	(8½ ounce) corn bread mix, prepared	1	(13½ ounce) can yellow cream style corn
1	cup shredded Cheddar cheese	1-2	jalapeño peppers, chopped
1	small red onion, chopped		

Preheat oven to 350 degrees. Prepare corn bread mix and add the remaining ingredients. Use a heavily oiled skillet or bread pan, pouring excess oil into corn bread mixture. Mix well. Bake for 50 minutes or until toothpick comes out clean.

Jewell Sims, Class of 1995

Sweet Potato Corn Bread

1	cup cooked and mashed sweet potatoes	1	cup oat flour or finely ground rolled oats
1¼	cups water	1	cup cornmeal
1	tablespoon safflower or canola oil	2	tablespoons cornstarch
1	teaspoon reduced-salt soy sauce	2	teaspoons baking powder
		2	teaspoons baking soda

Preheat oven to 400 degrees. In a food processor, blend sweet potatoes and water until the mixture is smooth. Put mixture into a large bowl. Add oil and soy sauce and stir until ingredients are blended. In a separate bowl, mix together remaining dry ingredients. With a spoon, stir dry ingredients into sweet potato mixture. Spread batter in a lightly oiled 9 x 9 inch non stick baking pan. Bake for 30 minutes, or until it begins to brown on top. Serve warm.

Josie Buckner, Class of 1992

We all love corn bread, but this recipe is perhaps the most healthy corn bread recipe of them all. It is sweetened only with sweet potatoes. This is one of my favorite recipes.

People think we're made up of Medicare, Social Security, doctor appointments, taking our medication on time. These things just aren't me. I have to deal with them, but inside I am the same man that served my country in the Army in World War II.

Graduate Class of 2000

Cheddar Nut Bread

1	egg, slightly beaten	3¾	cups buttermilk baking mix
1	cup undiluted evaporated milk	1½	cups shredded sharp Cheddar cheese
½	cup water	½	cup chopped nuts
¼	teaspoon salt		

Combine all ingredients. Mix vigorously 30 seconds or until blended. Spoon into buttered 9 x 5 x 3 inch loaf pan. Bake at 350 degrees for 55 to 60 minutes. Cool. Serve warm or cold.

Brenda Fowler, Friend of Senior Leaders

Zucchini Bread

3	eggs	¼	teaspoon baking powder
2	cups granulated sugar		
1	cup vegetable oil	¼	teaspoon baking soda
1	tablespoon vanilla	1	teaspoon salt
2	cups grated, peeled zucchini	1	cup walnuts, finely chopped
2	cups all-purpose flour	1	teaspoon grated lemon rind
1	teaspoon cinnamon		

In a large bowl, beat eggs until light and frothy. Add sugar, oil and vanilla mixing until thick. Add zucchini and stir thoroughly. In a separate bowl, sift together flour, cinnamon, baking powder, baking soda and salt. Stir into egg mixture until smooth. Add walnuts and lemon rind. Pour into 2 greased and floured loaf pans. Bake at 350 degrees for 1 hour. Remove from oven and cool for 15 minutes before turning out onto cooling rack.

Evelyn Cornelius, Class of 1993

In the 1970s, we planted our first "real" garden, although for several years we had grown "Corn Cob Tomatoes" and other oddities. We also planted peanuts so the children might see how the nuts grow underground. They were delighted over the little white "ghost nuts" that formed. This particular spring we planted zucchini, along with other vegetables, but had no idea that zucchini plants could be so prolific. Needless to say, we were inundated with beautiful bright green squash. After supplying the entire neighborhood, I was determined to find every possible use for zucchini. My mother helped by clipping recipes for me. It turned out to be my favorite of all the recipes I tried, and now I am seldom without zucchini bread in the freezer.

Sweet Potato Bread

⅓ cup shortening	1 teaspoon baking soda
¼ cup granulated sugar	½ teaspoon salt
2 eggs	½ teaspoon nutmeg
½ cup molasses	½ teaspoon cinnamon
1 cup cooked and mashed sweet potatoes	½ teaspoon allspice
	¼ teaspoon ground cloves
2 cups all-purpose flour	¼ cup raisins
¼ teaspoon baking powder	¾ cup chopped walnuts

Combine shortening, sugar and eggs. Beat until light and fluffy. Stir in remaining ingredients. Spread into a 9 x 5 x 3 inch loaf pan. Bake at 350 degrees for 1 hour.

Delores Taylor, Class of 1997

"LIFE Class helps elders like us to remember to be more careful in dealing with people. There are too many scam artists out there. I tell them 'I thank you, but I don't need anything done' because I am going to go find my own contractor."

LIFE Graduate

Banana Raisin Bread

1 cup brown sugar	½ cup oil or margarine
¾ cup granulated sugar	1 teaspoon vanilla
2 cups all-purpose flour	2 medium ripe bananas, mashed
1 teaspoon baking powder	
	2 snack sized boxes raisins
½ teaspoon salt	
2 eggs	

In a large bowl, sift together sugars. Add remaining dry ingredients. In a separate bowl, beat eggs lightly. Add oil, vanilla, mashed bananas and raisins. Add banana mixture to dry ingredients and mix well. Pour into a 5 x 9 inch loaf pan. Bake at 325 degrees for 35 to 40 minutes, or until cake pulls away from the sides.

Rosie Lee Green, Class of 1994

Be Sweet Banana Bread

2	cups all-purpose flour	½	teaspoon lemon extract
1	teaspoon baking soda	1	teaspoon vanilla extract
	Dash of salt	2	tablespoons milk
2	eggs	3	ripe bananas, mashed
⅓	cup oil	1	cup chopped walnuts
1	cup granulated sugar		

In a large bowl, sift together flour, baking soda and salt. In a separate bowl, combine eggs, oil and sugar. Add extracts and milk. Stir egg mixture into flour mixture. Fold in bananas and nuts. Pour into a greased loaf pan. Bake at 350 degrees for 30 minutes or until toothpick comes out clean.

Evelyn Cornelius, Class of 1993

Those of us in the 1993 LIFE class were very fortunate to get to know and love Luther Ballew. Mr. Ballew, at the age of 90, was a true gentlemen and an inspiration to all that came in contact with him. Banana nut bread was Mr. Ballew's favorite food. He remembered many happy times picnicking at Shelby Forest during the 1950s and 1960s when banana nut bread was always the picnic basket treat. He recalled the beautiful view from the high bluffs overlooking the river, and the large Persimmon tree which bore such sweet fruit in the fall. The recipe listed here was sampled by Mr. Ballew and he called it "the best in the world"! Since he was always cautioning us to be "sweet", we have named this the "Be Sweet Banana Nut Bread."

Self-Rising Banana Bread

¼	cup shortening	1	cup milk
1	egg	2	cups sliced or mashed
1	cup granulated sugar		bananas
1½	cups self-rising flour	¼	teaspoon vanilla

Mix shortening, egg and sugar until blended. Mix in flour alternately with milk. Add bananas and vanilla. Blend well. Pour into greased and floured 9 x 5 inch loaf pan. Bake at 350 degrees for 30 minutes.

Theresa Hudson, Class of 1992

Rich Holiday Banana Bread

1	stick butter	1	teaspoon baking soda
1	cup granulated sugar	3	bananas, mashed and
2	eggs		whipped until light
2	cups all-purpose flour	½	cup nuts

Cream butter and sugar. Beat in eggs one at a time. Add flour, baking soda and bananas. Stir in nuts. Pour into greased 9 x 5 inch loaf pan or 2 small loaf pans. Bake at 350 degrees for 45 minutes or until toothpick comes out clean. Remove from pan and cool on rack.

L. Almarita Johnson, Class of 1993

Note: Before the holidays, I begin to bake loaves of this bread for gifts. It freezes well, but let it stand overnight before freezing.

Monkey Bread

2	packages of yeast	3	eggs, beaten
¼	cup lukewarm water	3-4	cups all-purpose flour,
½	cup granulated sugar		sifted
1	cup milk	1	teaspoon salt
¼	pound butter		

Soften yeast in lukewarm water. Add sugar. Scald milk and add butter, allowing to melt. Cool to lukewarm. Add beaten eggs. Add yeast mixture. Add flour and salt. Mix well. Place in greased bowl and allow to rise. Roll out to ⅓ inch thickness. Cut with diamond cookie cutter and place in well oiled ring mold. Brush with melted butter and continue layering, brushing each layer with melted butter until mold is ¾ full. Allow to rise until double in bulk. Bake at 400 degrees until brown.

Note: A Bundt or tube cake pan may be used.

Grace Williams, Class of 1996

I first ate monkey bread when my best friend, Vera and I, along with our two preschool daughters visited Vera's aunt Julia in Los Angeles, California. Aunt Julia was a cook extraordinaire! She catered parties for the Hollywood stars. While serving us rare, exotic foods she entertained us with personal stories about the stars she had served. The stories nor the food impressed our girls until the day she presented them with their individual pans of monkey bread. After that visit out west, monkey bread became a family tradition in our family. I featured it in my foods column in the Tri-State Defender and monkey bread began to appear regularly on buffet tables around the city.

"LIFE classes are giving me confidence for things that I could do, when maybe when I was younger I would say I couldn't do them. A lady at church brought out her crocheting, that was one thing I always wanted to do. So I started taking up crocheting and when the first lady tried to teach me, she did such fancy work I went home and almost cried. And I said I will never be able to do that. But there was another lady there and she showed me. Last night I finished the first part of my Afghan. I learned I could do it too. Whatever I have learned in LIFE class, I always pass it on. I feel confident that I can go anywhere and talk to whomever I want to."

Graduate Class of 1999

Banana Nut Bread

¾	cup brown sugar	½	cup chopped walnuts or
¼	cup shortening		pecans
2	eggs	1	cup all-purpose flour
1	cup mashed ripe	2	teaspoons baking
	bananas		powder
¾	cup whole wheat or	½	teaspoon salt
	graham flour	¼	teaspoon baking soda

Preheat oven to 350 degrees. Grease a 9 x 5 x 3 inch loaf pan and set aside. Mix sugar, shortening and eggs in a bowl. Stir in bananas, whole wheat flour and nuts. In a separate bowl, combine all-purpose flour, baking powder, salt and baking soda. Add to banana mixture; mixing just until dry ingredients are moistened. Pour into loaf pan. Bake 1 hour, or until toothpick comes out clean. Remove from pan and cool on rack.

Betty Thompson, Class of 1994

Cakes

I value most my freedom.

Potneck

Do you know what Potneck is? Well few people do or will admit that they do. Have you heard of Golden Pond (not the Hepburn movie)? It is a place where the northwest corner of Stewart County joins northwest Kentucky at a bend of the Cumberland River. It was reported to be the home of the best "corn likker" ever made. That's what they say. I don't remember ever having tasted any.

The greater part of my young childhood was spent in what we called Potneck (Stewart County). We called the rolls that we made "ice box rolls" (see my recipe in the bread section of this cookbook). We actually used an icebox. We did not get an electric refrigerator 'til TVA came to Tennessee.

In the springhouse, we cooled the milk, butter, fruit and vegetables. Our farm had an artesian spring right out in a flat field. The spring branch was so cold, it made our hands and feet ache as we caught crawdads there. There we played a lot. Our grandparents built a neat little house across the branch (stream) as it left the spring. The timbers were hinged for the water to enter and exit. The bottom was filled with branch gravel, heavy timbers formed the side, and shelves lined the walls. Milk was kept in stone "crocks" or heavy metal "bushels." They were weighted by clean stones — didn't want to spill the beans or the milk.

I've been a city girl for a long time, well over 65 years. But I guess I am still the "Potnecker." — but now we were totally ignorant of "pot."

Novella Schulte, Class of 1995

Cheese Cake

1	layer Zwieback toast or 1 box Gerber toast	1	cup granulated sugar
4	egg whites	1	tablespoon vanilla
2	(8 ounce) packages Philadelphia cream cheese	2	cups sour cream
		2	tablespoons granulated sugar
		2	tablespoons vanilla

Make crumbs of toast and line bottom and sides of a well buttered spring bottom cake pan, reserving ½ crumbs for top. Preheat oven to 350 degrees. Beat 4 egg whites until very stiff. Cream together cream cheese, sugar and 1 tablespoon vanilla. Fold in egg whites very slowly until well blended. Pour into pan and bake for 25 minutes. Remove from oven and increase heat to 425 degrees. Mix together sour cream, 2 tablespoons sugar, 2 tablespoons vanilla and spread evenly on top, beginning at outer edges and working to center. Add reserved crust and put back in oven for 5 minutes. Cool to room temperature before removing from pan. Keep refrigerated. Prepare at least one day in advance before cutting.

Lorraine Kaufman, Senior Leaders Board of Directors

This recipe came from the old Villa restaurant on Perkins many years ago. Each Christmas I give one with cherry topping to each of some very close friends.

"Since LIFE class, I am more optimistic about aging, goal setting and really being active. I am optimistic about meeting the challenges of aging — really living the moment."

Grace Williams, Class of 1996

Abilene's Cake

½	cup butter	½	cup milk
1¼	cups granulated sugar	1	teaspoon vanilla
2	eggs	3	lemons
1½	cups all-purpose flour	¼	cup granulated sugar
1½	teaspoons baking powder		

Lightly grease and flour 9 inch tube pan and line with wax paper. Beat butter with sugar until light and fluffy. Add eggs, one at a time, beating after each addition. Sift flour with baking powder. Add flour mixture into butter mixture alternately with milk, beginning and ending with flour. Stir in vanilla. Pour into prepared pan and bake at 350 degrees for 35 to 40 minutes. In a sauce pan, mix lemon juice with sugar and warm over low heat. Remove cake from oven and turn off. Puncture cake with a long handled meat fork. Pour lemon sauce over cake and return to oven for 5 minutes. Cool and remove from pan.

Note: This is a very delicious and simple cake, which serves as a great base for fruit, ice cream or sauce. It is also very good sliced, buttered and toasted for breakfast.

Jean Watson, Class of 1992

When this special lady came into our family, she was probably in her late forties, but I am guessing, because she was ageless. She was a married woman without children. Abilene came to work first for my brother's family and then she started sharing her work week between that family and ours. Each family had 3 children. These 6 little cousins ranged in age from 5 years to 6 months. One of the children in one family was dangerously ill the first year of his life and one of the boys in the other family had Downs Syndrome. It was a busy time. Abilene walked to the door smiling and ready to lighten the burden for a weary mother. She changed her "bus" clothes and put on comfortable work clothes. Immediately she was picking up babies, changing diapers, dressing babies, feeding babies, talking to them and loving them. The next order of business was to get her cake in the oven. If you were lucky, you got to sit on the counter and watch her mix the cake. If you were really big and very, very lucky, you got to hold the mixer. Of course, she took care of the dads too and saw to it that dinner, including fresh turnip greens, was left on the back of the stove when her day was done. And then there was the time this mother's angel bundled up the two older boy cousins on a cold December morning and took them on an exciting bus ride "down town" to Goldsmith's to see the Enchanted Forest and Santa. Abilene stayed 6 years or maybe it was closer to 10. We all grew up. Abilene went to help someone else and we lost touch. However, there are pictures, memories, and there is "Abilene's Cake".

Ruby Witt's Pineapple Upside Down Cake

"Don't be afraid of us, we're just like you."

CAKE

1¼	cups cake flour	4	tablespoons butter, softened
1¼	teaspoons baking powder	1	egg, beaten
¼	tablespoon salt	½	cup milk
¾	cup granulated sugar		

TOPPING

½	cup brown sugar, firmly packed	4	pineapple slices
4	tablespoons butter		Cherries or pecans, optional
1	teaspoon vanilla		

Combine first 7 ingredients. Set aside. Mix together brown sugar, butter and vanilla. Spread into bottom of 9 inch baking pan. Place pineapple slices over topping. Place cherries or pecans in the center of each slice. Pour batter over pineapple layer. Bake at 350 degrees until firm and springs back in center.

Ruby Witt, Friend of Senior Leaders

In 1939, I got married and didn't know much about cooking. But I did make this cake for my new husband. He liked it so much that I kept one on the kitchen table at all times. If he finished the last piece at lunch, I would have another one ready for him when he returned home that evening. When my husband, Warren, Sr., came back home from World War II, I continued making this cake for him. He kidded about being "burned out" on it, but never stopped eating the ones I would fix for him. When our boys, Warren, Jr. and Gary, came along and began growing up, they joined their father in loving this special treat. So I guess you could say that Pineapple Upside Down Cake has been a tradition in the Witt family for several decades.

Pineapple Upside Down Cake

¼	cup margarine	1	(20 ounce) can crushed
½	cup brown sugar		pineapple, drained
		1	package carrot cake mix

Preheat oven to 350 degrees. In a 13 x 9 x 2 inch pan, heat margarine in oven until melted. Sprinkle sugar into melted margarine. Spoon pineapple over sugar. Prepare cake mix as directed on package. Pour over pineapple. Bake for 35 to 40 minutes. Cool 20 minutes. Invert on heat proof platter. Cool before serving.

Florene Allen, Class of 1995

I used to make this from scratch. It is nice to have an easier recipe.

Crumb Cake

2	cups packed brown sugar	½	cup chopped pecans
2½	cups all-purpose flour	1	cup milk
½	teaspoon salt	1	tablespoon baking
½	cup shortening or		powder
	butter, softened		Whipped topping
1	teaspoon cinnamon		Pecan halves, optional

Combine sugar, flour and salt. Cut in shortening until it resembles coarse meal. Set aside 1 cup of mixture and add cinnamon and nuts. To remaining crumb mixture, add milk and baking powder. Spread into greased 13 x 9 x 2 inch pan. Sprinkle with reserved crumb mixture. Bake at 350 degrees for 30 minutes or until cake tests done. Cut in squares. Garnish with whipped topping and pecans.

Georgia Bartosch, Class of 1992

Mama Mattie's Pound Cake

2	sticks butter	3	cups all-purpose flour, sifted
3	cups granulated sugar		
½	cup shortening	½	teaspoon baking powder
5	eggs		
1	cup milk	½	teaspoon vanilla

Preheat oven to 350 degrees. Cream butter, sugar and shortening in mixer. Add eggs, one at a time, mixing well after each addition. Stir in milk. Slowly mix in flour, baking powder and vanilla. Pour into large Bundt pan. Bake for 1 hour, or until toothpick comes out clean.

Cleo Merle Marthel, Friend of Senior Leaders

This recipe has been in my husband's family for many years. His grandmother has passed it down to the young ladies of the family so that our families can always enjoy it. It took me a few times to make it, to master it. When she first started teaching me how to make her pound cake, she would say, "Okay, you will need about a handful of this, and just keep putting that in until you get that right consistency. Little did she know I am the type of cook that needs measurements." Thank goodness she could come up with some measurements for me. She just looked at me and smiled. I hope you enjoy it as much as we do.

I learned in LIFE class that if I want assistance in the home should I need it, I'd better advocate for it now. In fact, by helping others remain at home, I am paving the way for my own independence.

Six Flavors Confectioners' Sugar Pound Cake

1	(1 pound) box confectioners' sugar	1	teaspoon almond flavoring
4	sticks margarine	1	teaspoon banana flavoring
6	eggs		
3	cups cake flour	1	teaspoon butter flavoring
1	teaspoon vanilla		
1	teaspoon lemon flavoring	1	teaspoon rum

Preheat oven to 350 degrees. Cream together sugar and butter. Alternately mix together 2 eggs and 1 cup flour until all is used. Add flavorings. Mix well. Pour into greased Bundt pan. Bake for 1 hour and 15 minutes.

Earline Washington, Class of 1995

Milky Way Cake

CAKE

8 Milky Way Bars
2 sticks butter
2 cups granulated sugar
4 eggs

2½ cups all-purpose flour
½ teaspoon baking soda
1¼ cups buttermilk
1 cup chopped pecans

ICING

2½ cups granulated sugar
1 cup evaporated milk
6 ounces semisweet
   chocolate chips

1 cup marshmallow cream
1 stick butter

Melt Milky Way bars with 1 stick butter. Set aside. Cream sugar and 1 stick butter. Add eggs. Add alternately flour, soda and buttermilk. Add melted bar mixture. Add pecans. Pour into tube pan. Bake at 325 degrees for 1 hour and 10 minutes, or until done. For icing, heat sugar and milk until soft. Add chocolate chips, marshmallow cream and butter. Stir until melted and of spreading consistency. Spread over cooled cake.

Yield: 10 servings

Peggy Byrd, Class of 1995

"When we sit down and listen to the younger people and sit there and hear them tell us what we can and can't do. So many times we hear our children say 'Oh, mom you are too old to do that.' I find myself telling them now, 'You CAN'T tell me what I can and can't do!'"

LIFE Graduate

Ma Bell's Coconut Cake

1	box white cake mix	1	(9 ounce) container
2	cups granulated sugar		Cool Whip
1	cup milk	1	(7 ounce) can flaked
1	teaspoon coconut		coconut
	flavoring		

Bake cake mix as directed in 9 x 13 inch pan. Cool. Mix together sugar and milk. Boil 1 minute. Remove from heat. Add flavoring. Punch holes in cake. Pour filling over entire cake. Cool. Spread Cool Whip over top and sprinkle with coconut. Keep refrigerated.

Marcie Harness, Class of 1995

Nelda's Sour Cream Chocolate Pound Cake

2	sticks butter	1	cup sour cream
3	cups granulated sugar	2	teaspoons vanilla
6	eggs, beaten	4	tablespoons cocoa
3	cups self-rising flour,		
	sifted twice		

Grease and flour Bundt pan. Cream butter and sugar. Add eggs. Stir in flour alternately with sour cream. When smooth, beat in vanilla and cocoa, one tablespoon at a time. Mix well on medium speed for 2 minutes. Pour into prepared pan. Bake at 325 degrees for 1 hour, or until toothpick comes out clean.

Nelda Grimes, Class of 1992

Chocolate Sheath Cake

CAKE

2	cups granulated sugar	1	cup buttermilk
2	cups all-purpose flour	1	teaspoon baking soda
1	stick butter	2	eggs, slightly beaten
½	cup shortening	1	teaspoon vanilla
4	tablespoons cocoa	1	teaspoon cinnamon
1	cup water		

ICING

1	stick butter	1	(1 pound) box
4	tablespoons cocoa		confectioners' sugar
6	tablespoons milk	1	teaspoon vanilla
		1	cup chopped nuts

Preheat oven to 400 degrees. Grease 11 x 16 inch pan. Sift together sugar and flour. Set aside. In a saucepan, mix butter, shortening, cocoa and water. Bring to boil then pour over flour mixture. Stir well. Add buttermilk, baking soda, eggs, vanilla and cinnamon. Mix well. Pour into prepared pan. Bake for 20 minutes. Five minutes before cake is done, bring butter, cocoa and milk to a boil. Remove from heat. Mix well. Add confectioners' sugar, vanilla and chopped nuts. Mix well. Pour over cake while cake and icing is still hot.

Betty Ball, Class of 1994

I think it was Mark Twain who said, "If you think you can or you think you can't, you're right." I think I can and LIFE class has reinforced this.

Peach Pound Cake

½	cup sour cream	3	cups all-purpose flour
2	cups chopped peaches	½	teaspoon salt
3	cups granulated sugar	1	teaspoon vanilla
2	sticks margarine	1	teaspoon almond
6	eggs		flavoring
½	teaspoon baking soda		

Combine sour cream, peaches, sugar and margarine. Cream until fluffy. Add eggs, one at a time. In a separate bowl, mix together baking soda, flour and salt. Add to creamed mixture. Add vanilla and almond flavoring. Bake at 350 degrees for 70 to 80 minutes.

Bess Bennett, Class of 1994

Buttermilk Pound Cake

1	cup butter, softened	½	teaspoon baking soda
2	cups granulated sugar	¼	teaspoon salt
4	eggs	1	cup buttermilk
3	cups all-purpose flour	2	teaspoons vanilla

Cream butter. Blend in sugar at medium speed until well blended. Add eggs, one at a time, beating after each addition. Combine flour, baking soda and salt. Add to creamed mixture alternately with buttermilk. Stir in vanilla. Pour into greased and floured tube pan. Bake at 325 degrees for 1 hour or until done. Cool in pan 10 minutes. Remove and cool completely.

Eloise Curtis, Class of 1994

Coconut Pound Cake

3	cups granulated sugar	3	cups cake flour
1	cup shortening	¼	teaspoon baking soda
6	eggs	2	teaspoons coconut
1	cup sour cream		flavoring

Cream sugar and shortening together until fluffy. Add eggs one at a time. Beat until smooth and creamy. Blend in sour cream. Sift together cake flour and baking soda. Add gradually to egg mixture until well blended. Add coconut flavoring. Pour into tube pan. Bake at 350 degrees for 1 hour or until toothpick comes out clean.

Victoria Smith, Class of 1994

Chocolate Pound Cake

1	cup butter	3	cups all-purpose flour
½	cup shortening	½	teaspoon baking powder
3	cups granulated sugar	½	teaspoon salt
5	eggs	4	tablespoons cocoa
1	teaspoon vanilla	1	cup milk

Cream together butter and shortening. Add sugar and mix well. Add eggs, one at a time, beating after each addition. Add vanilla. Combine dry ingredients and add alternately with milk to creamed mixture. Bake in greased 10-inch tube pan at 350 degrees for 80 minutes.

Bridget Ciaramitaro, Executive Director of Senior Leaders

I first started making this cake when my son was three years old. He would get on a stool and help with each step. He is now 14. Those moments are precious and I am happy every time he wants to cook. Children in the kitchen are a gift from God.

"When my daughter died, I just started staying at home doing nothing. Taking LIFE class has empowered me to go places and do things again. Remaining independent has become the most important thing to me and now I believe I can do it."

Earnestine Hughes, Class of 1999

Joy is dancing at any age.

Molasses Pound Cake

3	sticks butter, softened	1½	tablespoons ground ginger
1¼	cups firmly packed brown sugar	1	teaspoon ground nutmeg
6	eggs	½	teaspoon salt
5	cups sifted all-purpose flour	1½	teaspoons baking soda
1	tablespoon ground cinnamon	2	cups molasses
		½	cup milk

Cream butter and sugar until light and fluffy. Add eggs, one at a time, beating after each addition. Combine flour, spices and salt. Dissolve baking soda in molasses. Add dry ingredients to creamed mixture alternately with molasses and milk. Spoon in greased and floured 10-inch tube pan. Bake at 325 degrees for 1½ to 2 hours or until done. Cool in pan for 5 minutes. Turn out on cake rack to cool.

Jennie Morring, Class of 1993

In LIFE class, I met wonderful people. Another thing is I had just started working in the aging area and it was a wonderful opportunity for me to interact with other seniors as peers rather than in my role as a service provider. That was really great."

*Tommy Cervetti,
Class of 1994*

Vanilla Wafer Cake

2	sticks butter	2	cups flaked coconut
2	cups granulated sugar	1	cup finely chopped pecans
6	eggs		
½	cup milk	1	teaspoon vanilla, optional
4	cups crushed vanilla wafers		

Cream butter and sugar. Add eggs, one at a time, beating well after each addition. Add milk and wafers. Blend in coconut, nuts and vanilla. Pour into tube pan lined with four layers of waxed paper. Bake at 325 degrees for 75 minutes or until toothpick comes out clean.

Note: I have found with this recipe that any additional beating after the first three ingredients are added or using additional liquid will have negative results.

Dolores Taylor, Class of 1997

Jackson's Vanilla Wafer Fruit Cake

1	package Jackson's Vanilla Wafers	2	eggs, beaten well
1	pound pecans	½	cup white sugar
½	pound candied cherries	1	small can evaporated milk
½	pound candied pineapple	⅛	teaspoon salt
¼	pound white (golden) raisins (scant cup)		Spiced rum, optional
		2-3	slices of apple

Joy is making a scrapbook for your new granddaughter-in-law.

Crush vanilla wafers thoroughly. Set aside 4 whole cherries, 16 pecan halves and 2 slices of pineapple. Chop remaining fruit and nuts and add to vanilla wafer crumbs. In a large bowl mix together eggs, sugar, salt and milk. Stir in vanilla wafer mixture. Blend well. Let stand while preparing pan (use either a loaf or Bundt pan). Pack mixture firmly into pan. Decorate top with remaining cherries, pecan halves and pineapple. Bake at 325 degrees for 1 hour. Let completely cool and dribble on spiced rum. Place slices of apple on top of cake before wrapping to keep cake moist.

Betty Halstead, Class of 1995

The year of my first fruit cake was 1965. After that Christmas, the fruit cake became an annual event for my husband and me, and something different was added to one cake each time. Clyde (my husband) and I gather all the ingredients the week after Thanksgiving and I make my cakes within two weeks. I make three each year. These cakes are used on "goodie" trays, along with homemade chocolate fudge, roasted pecans ad whatever else I make. Then I distribute the trays to friends, relatives and a few shut-ins. This entire ritual came into being from that first fruit cake. It's something Clyde and I both look forward to and we've been doing it for 30 years!

Jam Cake

CAKE

1	cup shortening	1	cup buttermilk
2	cups granulated sugar	3	cups self-rising flour
4	eggs	1	teaspoon cinnamon
1	cup blackberry jam	1	teaspoon allspice
1	teaspoon baking soda	½	teaspoon salt

FILLING

1	small can crushed pineapple	⅓	cup water
		¼	cup butter
1½	cups granulated sugar	1	cup golden raisins
1	tablespoon all-purpose flour	1	cup chopped nuts
		1	cup coconut flakes

CARAMEL ICING

4½	cups granulated sugar, divided	1½	cups milk
		¾	cup butter
⅛	teaspoon salt	½	teaspoon vanilla

Cream shortening and sugar together until fluffy. Add eggs, one at a time, beating well after each addition. Add jam and mix well. Stir baking soda into buttermilk. Sift flour, spices and salt together. Add to jam mixture alternately with buttermilk. Grease and flour 3 (9-inch) cake pans. Pour batter into pans. Bake at 350 degrees for 25 to 30 minutes, or until toothpick comes out clean. Let cool in pan for 5 minutes. Remove and transfer to cooling rack. While cake is cooling, mix together pineapple, sugar, flour and water. Cook in heavy saucepan over medium heat until thickened, about 10 minutes. Remove from heat. Add butter, raisins, nuts and coconut. Set aside. For icing, mix together 3 cups sugar, salt and milk in a heavy saucepan over low heat stirring frequently. Meanwhile, place remaining sugar in iron skillet. Cook over medium heat until sugar dissolves and becomes brown and syrupy. Gradually pour into milk mixture. Remove from heat. Add butter and vanilla. Beat until thick enough to spread. When cake is cool spread filling between layers. Spread icing over top and sides.

Marilyn Baugus, Class of 1992

Dirt Cake

1	large package Oreo Cookies	3	cups milk
1	(8 ounce) package cream cheese	1	teaspoon vanilla
1	stick butter	1	large box vanilla instant pudding
1	cup confectioners' sugar	1	(12 ounce) container Cool Whip

Crush cookies in food processor until fine. In a large bowl, combine cream cheese, butter and sugar. Mix thoroughly. In a separate bowl, mix milk, vanilla and instant pudding. Beat until slightly thickened. Combine cream cheese mixture, pudding mixture and Cool Whip. Layer in a pan beginning with cookies and ending with cookies. Chill or freeze and serve.

Donovan Ciaramitaro (age 14), Friend of Senior Leaders

On Christmas Eve, everyone gathers at my house. Each year my mom and dad make lasagna. They started doing this long before I was born. On these special nights, I love to listen to everyone tell stories. They are funny, and I learn a lot about my family. A few years ago, I was at a church dinner and someone made Dirt Cake. I loved it! That Christmas I added this recipe to the Christmas Eve party. It's funny when you put it in a real flower pot and stick flowers in it! Who knows, maybe I will be telling stories and making Dirt Cake when I am old!

"LIFE is a program that I'm proud of. I've learned through this program how seniors may take their lives in stride without waiting for someone else to guide and mold their thoughts. We can do what we want to do. There is a secret that most LIFE graduates share, and that secret is empowerment."

Clyde Sanders, Class of 1994

Oreo Ice Cream Cake

1	(1 pound) package Oreo cookies	1	(12 ounce) jar hot fudge topping
⅓	cup melted butter	1	(12 ounce) container Cool Whip
½	gallon vanilla ice cream in a brick		

Freeze Oreo's overnight. Remove from freezer and place cookies 5 at a time into food processor. Process to fine crumbs. Pour into bowl. Mix melted butter into cookies. Stir until well blended. Butter bottom of 13 x 9 inch pan. Press ¾ of cookie mixture into bottom of pan. Open ice cream container on all sides. Slice into 6 even slices. Layer slices over cookie crumbs in pan. Smooth top with back of large spoon. Place in freezer immediately for 30 minutes. Warm hot fudge in microwave on low until liquid. Remove pan from freezer. Spoon fudge, 1 tablespoon at a time over ice cream, spreading evenly. Put back into freezer for 1 hour. Spread Cool Whip evenly over top. Sprinkle with remaining cookie mixture. Cover with plastic wrap and foil. Freeze overnight.

Note: It is important to place dish in the freezer so that it is level or the fudge will slide to one side.

JoAnn Davis, Enterprise National Bank

No one in my family buys ice cream cake anymore for birthdays and parties. This one is so much better. It tastes like an ice cream sundae and will serve a crowd of people. I got the recipe from someone I worked with a very long time ago and I've only made one small change to it. I've found that freezing the cookies before crushing them eliminates the sticky mess caused by mashing the filling. When my children were teenagers, I made one of these each week during the summer. My house was always filled with their friends!

Concrete Cake

CAKE

2	cups granulated sugar	3	eggs
3	cups self-rising flour	1	cup oil
½	cup cocoa	1	tablespoon vinegar
½	teaspoon salt	1½	cups milk
1	teaspoon baking soda	1	teaspoon vanilla

ICING

4	tablespoons margarine		Milk
4	tablespoons cocoa	1	teaspoon vanilla
2½	cups sifted confectioners sugar		

Preheat oven to 350 degrees. In a large bowl, combine dry ingredients. Beat eggs. Add oil and vinegar. Add dry ingredients to egg mixture, alternating with milk, beating well after each addition. Add vanilla and mix well. Grease Bundt pan and flour thoroughly. Pour batter into pan and bake for 45 minutes or until top springs back when touched. Remove from oven and let cool in pan for 10 minutes. Transfer to a dinner plate. Let cool completely. Mix together all ingredients for icing very slowly. Spread over top and sides of cake.

Georgia Bartosch, Class of 1992

This cake is an old recipe of my family's and my mother would make it for different occasions. It is one solid mass of chocolate dough and we loved it. We were all chocoholics, but we would tease Mother by asking, "What did you use to make this? You must have used concrete because it is so solid." So that's how it got its name.

"You know life ends sometime. You don't know how it's going to end. There's so many unexpected things and if you can keep a positive outlook, thinking of the more hopeful things and the prettier things, in a sense the pleasant things, you can have joy in the life you have left."

Mary Ruth Robinson, Senior Voices Participant

Vincent's Birthday Cake

"In LIFE Class, I got a totally new life style."

Judith Farmer, Class of 1995

CAKE

1	stick butter	1	teaspoon baking soda
½	cup vegetable shortening	1	cup buttermilk
		1	teaspoon vanilla
2	cups granulated sugar	1	cup chopped nuts
5	egg yolks	5	egg whites, stiffly beaten
2	cups all-purpose flour		

CREAM CHEESE FROSTING

1	(8 ounce) package cream cheese, softened	1	pound confectioners' sugar
½	stick butter	1	teaspoon vanilla
			Chopped pecans

Cream butter and shortening. Add sugar and beat until smooth. Add egg yolks and beat well. Combine flour and soda and add to creamed mixture alternately with buttermilk. Stir in vanilla. Add chopped nuts. Fold in stiffly beaten egg whites. Pour batter into 3 greased and floured 8 inch cake pans. Bake at 350 degrees for 25 minutes or until toothpick comes out clean. Cool completely. Beat cream cheese and butter until smooth. Add sugar and mix well. Add vanilla and beat until smooth. Spread between layers, on top and sides. Sprinkle with pecans or decorate if desired.

Bridget Ciaramitaro, Executive Director of Senior Leaders

In 1978, I wanted my husband's 30th birthday party to be special. Like most young people, he had begun to think of getting old and of all the things he had hoped to accomplish by then. I wanted him to think of his youth and all the opportunities ahead. He likes to have fun, so we planned a party for him with cake, hats, balloons, streamers and party whistles. The cake was the challenge. He just does not like many sweets. I searched and searched until I found this recipe. Not only did he love the party, he really loved the cake. Each year since then, I have been making this cake for his birthday. Sometimes there is a party and sometimes just the immediate family. I think he feels special because of this tradition. A few weeks ago he celebrated his 53rd birthday. It was the 23rd Italian Cream Cake. I hope when he celebrates his 100th birthday, I will be here to bake his cake.

Grandma's Cake

6	ounces chocolate chips	¾	cup oil
¼	cup all-purpose flour	¾	cup water
1	package yellow cake	4	eggs
	mix	¼	cup Vodka
1	(6 ounce) package	¼	cup Kahlúa
	instant chocolate		
	pudding mix		

Set aside chocolate chips and flour. Mix together remaining ingredients with blender until well blended. Mix flour with chips and fold into cake mix. Bake in greased Bundt pan at 350 degrees for 45 to 55 minutes, or until toothpick comes out clean.

Tommie Cervetti, Class of 1994

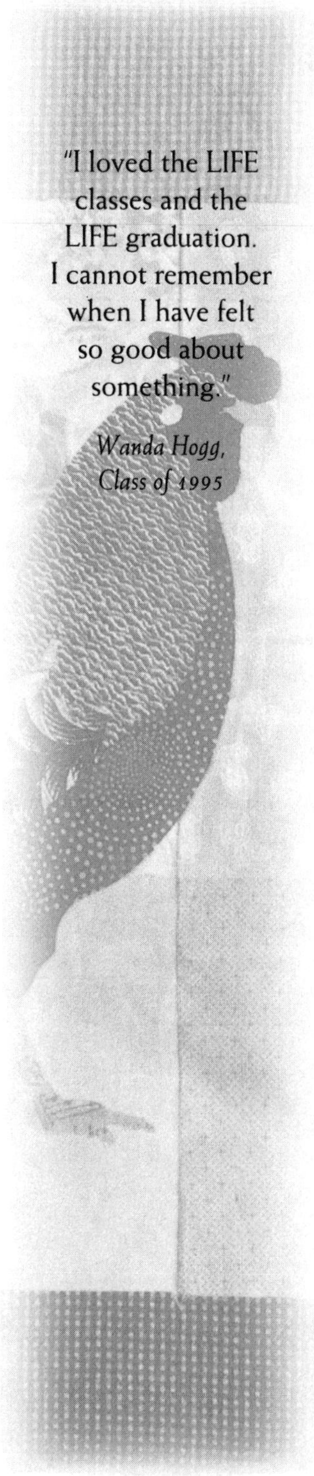

"I loved the LIFE classes and the LIFE graduation. I cannot remember when I have felt so good about something."

Wanda Hogg,
Class of 1995

Applesauce Cake

1	cup applesauce	⅛	teaspoon salt
⅞	cup brown or	1	teaspoon cinnamon
	granulated sugar	⅓	teaspoon powdered
⅓	cup oil		cloves
1¾	cups all-purpose flour	⅓	cup chocolate chips,
1	teaspoon baking soda		raisins or nuts

Preheat oven to 350 degrees. Mix together all ingredients and spoon into greased pan. Bake for 30 minutes.

Georgia Bartosch, Class of 1992

Strawberry Punch Bowl Cake

1	box yellow cake mix	2	cups granulated sugar
2	(21 ounce) cans strawberry pie filling	1	(20 ounce) can crushed pineapple, optional
2	(10 ounce) packages frozen sliced strawberries, thawed	2	cups chopped pecans, optional
		2	tubs Cool Whip

Bake cake as directed. Let cool. Break cake into large pieces. In a mixing bowl, combine pie filling, frozen strawberries, sugar, pineapple and pecans. In a punch bowl, layer ½ cake, ½ fruit mixture and ½ Cool Whip. Repeat. Refrigerate. Decorate with additional pecans and strawberries if desired. Best if prepared ahead and chilled. Serve using an ice cream scoop.

Yield: 15 servings

Laura Pounder, Class of 1998

Old-Fashioned Stack Cake

5½	cups all-purpose flour	1	cup granulated sugar
3	teaspoons baking soda	2	eggs, beaten
1	teaspoon cinnamon	2	cups molasses
1	teaspoon ginger	2	cups buttermilk
1	teaspoon salt		Applesauce
1	cup butter		

Sift together flour, baking soda, cinnamon, ginger and salt. In a separate bowl, cream butter and sugar. Add eggs, molasses, flour mixture and buttermilk. Beat until smooth. Pour into 3 shallow pans. Bake at 375 degrees for 20 minutes. Let cake cool. Spread applesauce between layers.

Helen Lockhart, Class of 1995

This wonderful recipe came from my mother's 1915 cookbook.

Cherry Punch Bowl Cake

1   box yellow cake mix
1   (6 ounce) package
    instant vanilla pudding
4   bananas, sliced
1   (20 ounce) can crushed
    pineapple, drained

1   (21 ounce) can cherry
    pie filling
1   (12 ounce) container
    Cool Whip
1   cup chopped nuts

Prepare cake and pudding according to directions. Layer in a punch bowl sliced cake, pudding, bananas, pineapple, pie filling and Cool Whip. Repeat layers until bowl is filled ending with Cool Whip. Sprinkle nuts over top.

Note: If you are making a large cake, double all ingredients except cake mix.

Charlie Lewis, Class of 1997

Chocolate Intrigue Cake

3   cups all-purpose flour
2   teaspoons baking
    powder
½   teaspoon salt
1   cup butter
2   cups granulated sugar

3   eggs
1   cup milk
1½   teaspoons vanilla
¾   cup chocolate syrup
¼   teaspoon soda
    Confectioners' sugar

Sift together flour, baking powder and salt. In a separate bowl, cream butter. Gradually add sugar. Blend well. Add eggs, one at a time, beating after each addition. Combine milk and vanilla and add alternately with dry ingredients. Turn ⅔ batter into well greased and lightly floured tube pan. Add to remaining batter chocolate syrup and baking soda. Mix well. Spoon chocolate batter over white batter. Do not mix. Bake at 350 degrees for 1 hour or until toothpick comes out clean. Dust lightly with confectioners' sugar.

Jane Christof, Class of 1996

Poor Folks Cake

CAKE

1½ cups granulated sugar	¼ teaspoon salt
¾ cup shortening	¼ teaspoon baking soda
2½ cups all-purpose flour	4 eggs
½ teaspoon baking powder	1 teaspoon flavoring of choice

FROSTING

1 cup confectioners' sugar	Lemon juice
¼ stick butter	

Cream sugar and shortening until smooth. Mix in remaining cake ingredients. Beat until it bubbles. With a mixer, mix frosting ingredients thoroughly. Pour batter into 2 greased and floured 9 inch cake pans. Bake at 350 degrees for 30 minutes or until toothpick inserted comes out clean. Remove from pan and cool completely. Spread on frosting and serve.

Josie Buckner, Class of 1992

When I was a little girl, we called this Poor Folks Cake because we had to put in whatever flavoring we had. Sometimes we used nutmeg or cinnamon.

"Because of the LIFE classes, I am now able to communicate my feelings, thoughts and opinions to my family, doctors and others. They always made decisions for me. I needed to make up my own mind, say "no" when I needed to. I felt a lot of growth. I now determine my own direction.

Geneva Burns, Class of 1996

Dump Cake

1 (20 ounce) can crushed pineapple	4 ounces raisins
½ cup brown sugar	1 cup chopped walnuts or pecans
1 package cake mix	2 sticks butter, sliced

In a buttered 9 x 13 inch pan, dump in pineapple followed by sugar, cake mix, raisins, nuts and top with butter. Bake at 300 degrees for 75 minutes.

Teresa Lewis, Class of 1997

Coconut Sour Cream Cake

CAKE

1	box white cake mix
3	eggs
1	(8 ounce) carton sour cream

¼	cup oil
1	(8½ ounce) can cream of coconut

ICING

1	(8 ounce) package cream cheese
2	tablespoons milk

1	pound confectioners' sugar
1	teaspoon vanilla
¾	cup Angel Flake Coconut

Mix together cake ingredients in electric mixer. Pour into greased 9 x 13 inch pan and bake at 350 degrees for 30 to 45 minutes or until toothpick comes out clean. Let cool completely. Blend together icing ingredients thoroughly and spread over cake. Sprinkle with coconut on top and pat on sides. Keep refrigerated.

Tommie Cervetti, Class of 1994

This recipe was given to me by my sister-in-law from Little Rock. Everyone loves it!

Joy is sharing a rich dessert with a friend so that both can enjoy but neither over does it.

Cheesecake

4 (8 ounce) packages cream cheese, room temperature	1¼ cups granulated sugar
	¼ pound unsalted butter, room temperature
16 ounces sour cream, room temperature	6 eggs, room temperature
2 tablespoons cornstarch	1 10-inch springform pan
1 teaspoon lemon juice	Roasting pan for water bath
1¼ teaspoons vanilla	

Preheat oven to 375 degrees. Grease bottom of spring form pan. Set aside. In a large mixing bowl, beat cream cheese, adding one package at a time, until smooth and creamy. Add sour cream and beat until smooth. Add cornstarch, lemon juice, vanilla, sugar and butter. Continue beating at low speed until smooth. Do not over beat butter or it will separate. Add eggs, one at a time, beating well after each addition. Pour batter into springform pan. Place pan inside roasting pan. Pour warm water into roasting pan until it reaches half way up cake pan. Place in oven and bake 1 hour. Remove from oven and cool in pan 2 hours. Refrigerate over night. Unlock outer ring of pan and remove cake. Decorate or leave plain. Keep refrigerated.

JoAnn Davis, Enterprise National Bank

This was my stepmother's signature dish. Everyone begged for her cheesecake, the smooth, rich, famous New York Cheesecake. No crust, just solid, melt-in-your-mouth cheesecake. She had a combined family of 9 children, and many more grandchildren, so we all kept her very busy. She very generously shared her recipe with me and now this is my most asked for dish.

Apple Cake

1½	cups oil	1	teaspoon salt
2	cups granulated sugar	1	teaspoon baking soda
2	eggs	2	teaspoons baking
1	teaspoon vanilla		powder
2½	cups sifted all-purpose	3	cups apples, chopped
	flour	1	cup pecans

In a large bowl, combine oil, sugar, eggs and vanilla. Beat until creamy at low speed. Sift together flour, salt, baking soda and baking powder. Gradually add to egg mixture. Mix well. Fold in apples and pecans. Pour into a 9 x 13 pan lined with waxed paper. Bake at 350 degrees for 55 minutes.

Lou Thompson, Class of 1995

This recipe was passed down to me from my mother-in-law. She baked it for her grandchildren on special occasions. Even today they request it when they come home. I love to use it for special occasions when I need a good dessert.

Joy is coming home from the doctor and being greeted by Sweetie Pie, the dog.

Fast-Fixin' Double Banana Cake

¼	cup oil	½	cup chopped nuts,
1	package banana cake		optional
	mix	2	eggs
2	medium-size ripe	1	cup water
	bananas, mashed	⅓	cup granulated sugar

Preheat oven to 350 degrees. Pour oil into 13 x 9 x 2 inch pan, tilting pan to cover bottom. In a bowl, combine remaining ingredients, stirring with a fork or spoon until blended, about 2 minutes. Scrape sides and spread batter evenly in pan. Bake 35 to 45 minutes, or until toothpick inserted near center comes out clean. Cooled cake may be sprinkle with powdered sugar. Use knife to loosen cake from sides. Cut and serve directly from pan. Store cake loosely covered.

Sandra Engelhardt, Friend of Senior Leaders

Strawberry Cake

My goal is to live life fully until the very moment I draw my last breath. A full life has ups and downs, joys and sorrows. I do not want to miss out on a single one.

CAKE

1	box white cake mix	4	eggs
1	box strawberry jello	½	cup frozen strawberries,
¾	cup oil		thawed and drained
½	cup water		

ICING

½	cup frozen strawberries	1	pound confectioners'
1	stick margarine		sugar
		½	teaspoon salt

Mix together cake mix, jello, oil and water. Beat well. Add eggs, one at a time, beating after each addition. Add strawberries and beat well. Pour into 9 x 13 inch baking pan. Bake at 350 degrees for 25 minutes. For icing, thaw strawberries reserving juice. Blend together margarine, sugar, salt, strawberries and juice. Spread icing over cooled cake.

Bobby Ruth McCaskill, Class of 1995

This was our "family cake." I remember making this for the kids and they would take it to school to show off.

Red Velvet Cake

CAKE

2	eggs	1	teaspoon vanilla
1½	cups granulated sugar	2½	cups self-rising flour
1½	cups oil	1	cup buttermilk
1	ounce red food coloring		

ICING

1	(8 ounce) package cream cheese, softened	1	pound confectioners' sugar
1	stick butter, softened	1	teaspoon vanilla
		1	cup pecans, chopped

In a large bowl, cream eggs and sugar. Add cooking oil, food coloring and vanilla. Mix well. Add flour alternately with buttermilk. Beat well. Pour into three 9 inch cake pans lined with wax paper. Bake at 375 degrees 20 to 25 minutes or until cake pulls away from sides. Turn out cakes upside down on a cooling rack. For icing, mix together cream cheese and butter. Add confectioners' sugar. Mix well. Stir in vanilla and pecans. Spread icing between layers, over top and sides.

Note: For Christmas, I make green icing by adding green food coloring to desired color.

Lucille Vescova, Class of 1992

This cake made by this cook is absolutely divine. - Bridget Ciaramitaro

Children in today's world have so much, but they may be missing some of the simplest pleasures — the sweet smell of a towel dried on an outdoor clothes line, sitting around the fire listening to stories of times past, eating bread cooked in a wood stove, riding in the snow in a one horse sleigh.

Lemon Kiss Cake

CAKE

1	package yellow cake mix	1	(3 ounce) package lemon gelatin dessert
¾	cup salad oil	3	eggs
¾	cup water	½	teaspoon salt
1	teaspoon lemon extract or fresh lemon juice		

GLAZE

1	cup confectioners' sugar	1	lemon, juiced
2	tablespoons melted butter		

Combine cake mix, oil, water, lemon extract and gelatin. Add eggs and salt. Beat well. Pour into oiled and floured 10 inch tube cake pan. Bake at 350 degrees for 45 minutes. In a small bowl, combine sugar, butter and lemon juice. Remove hot cake from pan and glaze.

Brenda Fowler, Friend of Senior Leaders

The best thing that ever happened to me was family.

Ice Cream Crunch Pie

PIE

3	cups crisp rice cereal	¾	cup chocolate chips
½	cup chopped Brazil nuts, toasted	2	tablespoons butter
		2	pints vanilla or coffee ice cream

TOPPING

1	package powdered dessert topping mix	2	tablespoons hot chocolate powder
1	tablespoon instant coffee		Cocoa powder, optional

Mix cereal and nuts in a greased bowl. Melt chocolate chips and butter in a double broiler and stir. Pour over cereal-nut mixture. Spread in deep, greased 9 inch pie plate. Chill. Fill with ice cream, pressing down evenly with the back of a warm spoon. Prepare the dessert topping according to package instructions. Beat in coffee and chocolate powder. Spread over ice cream. Sprinkle lightly with cocoa powder if desired. Freeze until firm.

Yield: 8 servings

Mal Shapiro, Class of 1994

As a seaman in the Merchant Marines, one of my assignments in 1945 was on a luxury liner Mariposa (Spanish for butterfly). This was quite an improvement from the Liberty and Victory ships which had been rushed into duty in WW II to carry a variety of allied soldiers to the war fronts and back. The Mariposa crew often recalled carrying Sengalese troops early in 1943. I made two trips to Australia on the Mariposa, bringing war brides and their children to San Francisco. My most memorable voyage was in September, 1945, when we returned Brazilian army units from Naples, Italy to Rio. Brazil was an interesting destination, from the Christ of the Andes overlooking Rio to the Brazil nut trees which, when grown along the Amazon, sometimes reached heights of 150 feet and 6 feet in diameter. The spherical fruit, or seed, is about 6 inches in diameter and contains about 20 of the triangular nuts. Some of the products identified with Brazil (coffee, chocolate and Brazil nuts) are included in this recipe.

Fried Pies

CRUST
⅓ cup shortening
1½ cups self-rising flour

⅓ cup ice water
Oil

CHOCOLATE FILLING
¼ cup granulated sugar
¼ cup self-rising flour
1 tablespoon cocoa
   powder

½ cup milk
2 tablespoons butter
½ teaspoon vanilla

FRUIT FILLING
2 cups dried fruit
1¾ cups water

½ cup granulated sugar, or
   to taste
¼ cup butter

To make crust, cut shortening into flour until crumbly. Add ice water until flour mixture holds together. If needed add more water, 1 teaspoon at a time. Roll out on lightly floured board. Cut into 6 inch diameter rounds. For chocolate filling, combine sugar, flour and cocoa in a heavy saucepan. Stir in milk and butter. Cook over medium heat, stirring constantly until thickened and smooth, 3 to 5 minutes. Remove from heat. Stir in vanilla. Cool completely before making pies. For fruit filling, wash fruit and cover with water. Bring to boil, and cook for 15 minutes. Add sugar. Cook 5 more minutes, stirring often to prevent sticking. Remove from heat. Add butter. Let cool. Place 2 tablespoons of filling of choice in center of each round. Fold over crust in half. Moisten edges and press together with tines of fork. In skillet, fry in 2 inches of oil for 3 minutes. Turn and fry an additional 3 minutes.

Marilyn Baugus, Class of 1992

My mama made her pie crust rounds the size of a small plate and two fitted exactly into a 9 inch black skillet. My brother-in-law makes the chocolate pies and keeps them in the freezer to take deer hunting.

"LIFE has something for all seniors. For myself I have gotten to be a better public speaker and more empowered to get what I want."

Mary Locke
LIFE Class of 1999,
Philadelphia

Apples Plus Love

2	(9 inch) unbaked pie crust	½	teaspoon cinnamon
6	cups apples, sliced	½	teaspoon nutmeg
¾	cups plus 1 teaspoon granulated sugar	1	teaspoon all-purpose flour
		½	stick butter, melted

Combine apples, ¾ cup sugar, cinnamon, nutmeg and flour. Pour ingredients into 1 crust. Dot with butter. Cut remaining crust into ¾ inch strips. Lay strips across pie in a lattice pattern. Brush top crust with melted butter and sprinkle with sugar. Bake at 450 degrees for 30 to 45 minutes.

Joyce F. Johnson, Friend of Senior Leaders

Mudear's performance in the kitchen was not quite as skillful as on the piano. She often tried her favorite recipes like vegetable soup, turnip greens and her famous "apple pie with love". She said, "It's hard to mess up apples." However, there were more times when she did just that. She had a habit of amusing herself on the piano while waiting for her pies to bake and inevitably too much time would pass and they would "overcook." That never discouraged my living, spry, darling 80 year old young mother. She would just start over again. When I have tried this recipe, it never turned out as tasty as hers, even the burned ones.

Favorite Apple Pie

1 cup all-purpose flour
1½ teaspoons granulated
    sugar
¼ cup margarine
2-3 tablespoons cold water
    Vegetable cooking spray
4¼ cups peeled, sliced
    apples
2 tablespoons lemon juice
⅓ cup granulated sugar

2 tablespoons all-purpose
    flour
½ teaspoon ground
    cinnamon
⅛ teaspoon ground nutmeg
¼ cup all-purpose flour
3 tablespoons brown sugar
1 tablespoon margarine
⅛ teaspoon ground
    cinnamon

Combine flour and sugar. Cut in margarine with pastry blender until it resembles coarse meal. Sprinkle in cold water, 1 tablespoon at a time. Stir with fork until dry ingredients are moistened. Shape dough into ball. Cover and chill 10 minutes. Roll dough between 2 sheets of heavy-duty plastic wrap to a 12 inch circle. Place in freezer for 10 minutes until plastic wrap can be removed easily. Remove top sheet of plastic wrap. Invert into pie plate coated with cooking spray. Remove remaining sheet. Fold edges under and flute. In a large bowl, combine apples and lemon juice. Toss gently to coat. Combine sugar, flour, cinnamon and nutmeg. Stir well. Sprinkle over apple mixture, toss gently and spoon into pastry shell. Set aside. In a small bowl, combine flour, brown sugar, margarine and cinnamon. Stir well. Sprinkle evenly over apple mixture. Bake at 425 degrees for 20 minutes. Cover edges of pastry with strips of aluminum foil. Bake an additional 10 minutes.

Symeria K. Clemons, Class of 2000

Lemon Pie

4	eggs	1	tablespoon melted
⅔	cup granulated sugar		butter
6	tablespoons milk		Pie Crust (see below)
1	lemon, juiced		

Combine 4 egg yolks and 2 egg whites with sugar, milk, lemon juice, 1 teaspoon lemon rind and butter. Pour into pie crust. Bake at 350 degrees for 30 minutes. Beat remaining 2 egg whites and top cooked pie. Place in oven until meringue is lightly browned.

Marilyn Wilson, Friend of Senior Leaders

Pie Crust

1	cup all-purpose flour	1	cup all-purpose flour
⅔	cup shortening	¼	cup water
1	teaspoon salt		

Mix 1 cup flour, shortening and salt. Add in 1 cup flour and water. Mix well. Roll out.

Yield: 2 crusts

Marilyn Wilson, Friend of Senior Leaders

Lemon Meringue Pie

1	(9 inch) pie shell, baked	⅓	cup lemon juice
1	cup granulated sugar	2	teaspoons grated lemon
6	tablespoons cornstarch		rind
½	teaspoon salt	¼	teaspoon cream of tartar
2	cups water	4	tablespoons granulated
3	eggs, separated		sugar
3	teaspoons butter	½	teaspoon vanilla

In a saucepan, combine sugar, cornstarch, salt and water. Cook, stirring constantly, over low heat until thickened. Transfer to a double boiler, cover and cook for 10 minutes. Remove from heat. Add ½ cup of mixture to beaten egg yolks. Add yolks to sugar mixture and cook for 3 minutes, stirring constantly. Remove from heat. Add butter, lemon juice and lemon rind. Cool and pour into pie shell. Beat together egg whites, cream of tartar, sugar and vanilla until stiff peaks form. Spread over pie filling. Bake at 325 degrees until brown.

Shirley Minor, Class of 1992

Seminary Kentucky Pie

½	cup Karo syrup, light or dark	1	cup brown sugar
½	cup Molasses	½	stick butter
3	eggs, slightly beaten	1	cup pecans or walnuts
⅛	teaspoon salt	½	cup semisweet
1	teaspoon vanilla		chocolate chips
1-2	tablespoons Makers Mark bourbon	1	(9 inch) pie shell, unbaked

Preheat oven to 400 degrees. Combine all ingredients well, adding nuts and chocolate chips last. Pour into pie shell. Bake at 400 for 15 minutes. Reduce oven heat to 350 degrees and bake 30 to 35 minutes longer. When pie is done, outer edges of the filling should be set, with the center slightly soft. Remove from oven, cook and serve with fresh whipping cream or ice cream if desired.

Bridget Ciaramitaro, Executive Director, Senior Leaders

Best Ever Caramel Pie

1½	cups granulated sugar	3	eggs, separated
1	cup hot water	1	teaspoon vanilla
3	tablespoons all-purpose flour	1	(9 inch) pie shell, baked
1	(12 ounce) can evaporated milk	3	tablespoons granulated sugar

Melt and brown ¾ cup sugar in heavy iron skillet. Shake skillet to keep sugar from burning. Once brown, add hot water and simmer until dissolved. In a separate pan, mix ¾ cup sugar with flour. Stir in ½ of milk. Add egg yolks and remaining milk. Mix well. Gradually add caramelized syrup and cook over medium heat, stirring constantly until thickened. Add vanilla. Cool. In a bowl, beat egg whites until stiff. Add sugar and continue to beat until stiff peaks form. Pour filling into crust. Cover with meringue. Bake at 350 degrees until golden brown.

Evelyn Cornelius, Class of 1993

My mother and two older sisters were all good cooks. I can remember enjoying this pie many times while growing up. My sister still makes caramel pie for me on special occasions. She once brought a whole pie for me to give to my best friend on her birthday. She declared it the best birthday gift ever! "Fat" doesn't enter into the picture when it comes to caramel pie!

Fudge Pie

2 (1 ounce) squares bitter
   sweet chocolate
1 stick margarine

¼ cup sifted all-purpose
   flour
1 cup granulated sugar
2 eggs

Melt chocolate and margarine in a double boiler. In a small bowl, combine flour and sugar. In a large bowl, beat eggs. Add flour and chocolate mixtures. Pour into well greased pie tin. Bake at 350 degrees for 30 to 40 minutes. Serve with whip cream or ice cream.

Carolyn Vester, Owner of WOW Fashions

Mama's Kitchen
(January 19, 1931 – June 18, 1998)

The sweet smell of pies a baking

The stove set to make them rise.

A sweet aroma thru out the house

Oh boy! It was mama's pies.

Not a lot of mushy stuff,

Such as always "huggin" and "kissin".

But love was always there

Each time Mama was in the kitchen.

Four Layer Chocolate Pie

1 cup all-purpose flour	1 cup confectioners' sugar
1 stick margarine	1 cup Cool Whip
½ cup chopped pecans	2 small packages instant
1 (8 ounce) package cream	chocolate pudding
cheese, softened	3 cups milk

Cream together flour and margarine. Press into bottom of 9 x 12 inch dish. Sprinkle with pecans and press them into crust. Bake at 325 degrees for 25 minutes. Cool completely. Combine cream cheese, sugar and Cool Whip. Mix until smooth and creamy. Spread evenly over crust layer. Combine pudding and milk. Mix until smooth and thick. Spread over cream cheese layer. Top with remaining Cool Whip. Refrigerate several hours before serving.

Catherine Bailey, Class of 1995

Diabetic Apple Pie

4 cups sliced apples	½ teaspoon lemon juice
½ cup apple juice from	½ teaspoon cinnamon
concentrate	½ teaspoon nutmeg
2 teaspoons all-purpose	2 (9 inch) pie crusts
flour	

Mix all ingredients together. Pour into prepared pie shell. Top with second crust. Bake at 425 degrees for 40 to 45 minutes.

Pat Doty, Class of 1994

Chocolate Chess Pie I

1	stick butter	1	teaspoon vanilla
2	(1 once) squares semi-		Dash salt
	sweet chocolate	1	(9 inch) unbaked pie
2	eggs, slightly beaten		shell
1	cup granulated sugar		

Preheat oven to 350 degrees. Melt butter and chocolate. In a separate bowl, blend together eggs, sugar, vanilla and salt. Blend egg mixture with chocolate mixture. Pour into pie shell. Bake 35 minutes. Serve warm with whipped cream or ice cream.

Bill Ramsey, Friend of Senior Leaders

Chocolate Chess Pie II

1½	cups granulated sugar	2	teaspoons vanilla
3	tablespoons cocoa	2	eggs
½	stick butter	1	(9 inch) unbaked pie
⅔	cup evaporated milk		shell

Mix all ingredients and pour into pie shell. Bake at 350 degrees for 30 to 40 minutes or until firm. Do not overcook.

Evelyn Buford, Class of 1997

I am diabetic, but I enjoy baking and sharing with friends. I also enjoy taking my many treats to church dinners or potlucks. This pie is a favorite of the Senior Leader gang. By sharing with others, I can still bake and not be tempted to eat the sweets myself. Of course, I do give my husband a little taste!

Peanut Butter Cream Pie

½	cup peanut butter	3	eggs, separated
¾	cup confectioners' sugar	3	cups milk
⅔	cup granulated sugar	2	tablespoons butter
3	tablespoons cornstarch	1	teaspoon vanilla
1	tablespoon all-purpose flour	1	(9 inch) pie shell
⅓	teaspoon salt	¼	teaspoon cream of tartar
		¼	cup granulated sugar

Cream peanut butter and confectioners' sugar until crumbly. Set aside. In a large saucepan, mix sugar, cornstarch, flour, salt, beaten egg yolks, milk, butter and vanilla. Cook over medium heat, stirring constantly, until thick. Sprinkle ⅔ of peanut butter mixture into pie shell. Pour filling over that. For meringue, beat egg whites and cream of tartar until stiff. Gradually add sugar, beating well. Spread meringue over filling. Sprinkle with remaining peanut butter mixture. Bake at 350 degrees until golden brown.

Marilyn Baugus, Class of 1992

Basic Pie Crust

½	cup shortening	4-5	tablespoons ice water
1½	cups self-rising flour		

Cut shortening into flour with pastry blender until the consistency of coarse meal. Add water, 1 tablespoon at a time, until flour is moistened. Roll out on floured surface to fit pie pan. Prick holes in crust with fork and bake at 400 degrees for 10 minutes, or until brown.

Yield: 2 (9 inch) crusts

Marilyn Baugus, Class of 1992

Buttermilk Pie

1	(9 inch) baked pie shell	⅔	cup buttermilk
4	eggs	½	cup margarine
2	cups granulated sugar	1	teaspoon vanilla
2	tablespoons all-purpose flour		

Mix all ingredients well. Pour into 2 prepared pie shells. Bake at 350 degrees for 35 minutes or until pie is firm in center.

Yield: 2 pies

Sara Reed-Dixon, Class of 1997

Joy is finding one of those little scooters at the grocery store.

Shoo Fly Pie

¾	cup all-purpose flour	¼	teaspoon salt
½	cup firmly packed brown sugar	2	tablespoons shortening
½	teaspoon ground cinnamon	½	cup molasses
⅛	teaspoon ground cloves	¾	cup boiling water
⅛	teaspoon ground ginger	1½	teaspoons baking soda
⅛	teaspoon ground nutmeg	1	egg yolk, well beaten
		1	(9 inch) pie shell, baked

Mix together first 7 ingredients. Cut in shortening until crumbly. Set aside. Combine remaining 4 ingredients. Alternate layers of crumbs and liquid mixture in pie shell finishing with crumbs. Bake at 450 degrees for 10 minutes. Reduce to 350 degrees and bake 20 minutes or until firm.

Teresa Lewis, Class of 1997

The story behind the name. A group of Amish women were making pies in the yard on a work table. The flies were bad in the area where they were working. They kept saying "Shoo fly! Shoo fly!" Thus the Pennsylvania Dutch dessert, Shoo Fly Pie.

Grandma Leo Keeter's Coconut Cream Pie

3	eggs, separated	1⅓ cups coconut
2	cups milk	1 (9 inch) pie shell, baked
⅓	cup granulated sugar	½ teaspoon vanilla
⅓	cup all-purpose flour	¼ teaspoon cream of tartar
¼	teaspoon salt	6 tablespoons granulated
2	teaspoons butter	sugar
1	teaspoon vanilla	

Preheat oven to 350 degrees. In a medium saucepan, combine egg yolks and milk. Mix well. Add sugar, flour and salt. Cook over medium heat until thick, stirring constantly. Remove from heat. Add butter, vanilla and 1 cup coconut. Pour into baked pie crust. Beat egg whites with vanilla and cream of tartar until soft peaks form. Gradually add sugar. Beat until stiff. Spread meringue over filling. Sprinkle with remaining coconut. Bake 12 to 15 minutes or until brown.

Gayle Toland, Class of 1995

Grandma Leo Keeter is my mother. Years ago, my granddaughters made a cookbook of Grandma's recipes with family pictures: Grandma and Grandpa in the kitchen, family shots of their parents and childhood pictures. In 1978, there was a family reunion in Dallas, and this Coconut Cream Pie was served. This recipe was published in the Dallas Morning News in a report about the reunion. Relatives in Portland, Oregon and New Jersey have found the recipe published in their areas, too. My mother lived to be 94.

Karo Pecan Pie

3 eggs
1 cup Karo syrup, light or
   dark
½ teaspoon salt
1 teaspoon vanilla

½ cup granulated sugar
¼ cup melted butter
½ cup pecans
1 (9 inch) baked pie crust

Beat together eggs, syrup, salt, vanilla, sugar and butter. Line the bottom of crust with pecans. Pour filling over pecans. Bake at 350 degrees for 50 to 60 minutes.

Jeannie Bowles, Class of 1995

I only make this pie for those Christmas' when the whole family gets together. Sometimes that's only once every 3 to 4 years. But when we do, I wind up cooking for 6 children and 20 grandchildren. And they all look forward to my pecan pie when they come home. That's the only time of year they will get it so it is a very special treat.

"Change is not necessary to life, it is life. This experience in LIFE class is the simple most wonderful, valuable thing I have ever done for myself."

*Dolores,
LIFE Class of 1999,
Philadelphia*

Million Dollar Pie

1 (14 ounce) can
   sweetened condensed
   milk
1 (15 ounce) can crushed
   pineapple

1 (9 ounce) container
   Cool Whip
3 lemons, juiced
1 cup chopped pecans
2 graham cracker pie crusts

Mix all ingredients together well. Pour into crusts. Refrigerate for at least 2 hours.

Rosemary Hill, Class of 1998

Blackberry Cobbler

1	quart blackberries	1½	cups self-rising flour
1½	cups granulated sugar	¼	cup ice water
2	tablespoons all-purpose flour	4	tablespoons butter
4	tablespoons butter	2	tablespoons granulated sugar
½	cup shortening		

Place blackberries in a 9 inch baking pan. Mix sugar and flour. Sprinkle over berries. Dot with butter. Set aside. Cut shortening into flour. Add ice water until mixture is well moistened and holds together. Add more if needed. Roll out on floured surface. Fit over berries. Dot with butter. Sprinkle with sugar. Bake at 350 degrees for 40 to 45 minutes, until crust is brown.

Marilyn Baugus, Class of 1992

Egg Custard Pie

3	eggs	¾	stick margarine, melted
1	cup granulated sugar	2	teaspoons vanilla
1	tablespoon all-purpose flour	1	(9 inch) deep dish pie crust, baked
1	(13 ounce) can evaporated milk		

In a large bowl, beat eggs well. In a separate bowl, mix flour with sugar. Stir into eggs. Add milk and margarine. Mix well. Stir in vanilla. Pour into unbaked pie shell. Bake at 325 degrees for 55 to 60 minutes, or until toothpick comes out clean.

Willie Pearl Johnson, Class of 1995

Whiskey Chess Pie

4	eggs	¾	stick butter, melted
1½	cups granulated sugar	1	(9 inch) unbaked pie
1	tablespoon vinegar		shell
3	tablespoons bourbon		
	whiskey		

Combine all ingredients. Pour into pie shell. Bake at 325 degrees for 30 minutes or until light brown and pie is firm in center.

Jennie Morring, Class of 1993

Mama's Chocolate Pie

1	(9 inch) baked pie shell	1	teaspoon vanilla
¾	cup granulated sugar	3	tablespoons butter,
2	tablespoons all-purpose		melted
	flour	¼	teaspoon cream of tartar
3	tablespoons cocoa	3	tablespoons granulated
1½	cups milk		sugar
2	egg yolks	3	egg whites

Mix sugar, flour and cocoa in saucepan. Add milk. Mix well. Beat egg yolks and add to mixture. Cook until thick, stirring constantly. Remove from heat. Add vanilla and butter. Pour into prepared pie crust. In a mixing bowl, blend together cream of tartar, sugar and egg whites. Beat until stiff peaks form. Cover pie with meringue. Bake at 350 degrees until golden brown.

Rowena Stephens, Class of 2000

Egg Pie

1½ cups granulated sugar ½ stick butter
1 tablespoon cornstarch 1 teaspoon vanilla
4 eggs Nutmeg to taste
1 tall can evaporated milk

Beat sugar, cornstarch, eggs and milk. Add butter, vanilla and nutmeg. Bake at 350 degrees for 40 to 45 minutes or until pie is firm in center. Do not overcook.

Mattie Toliver, Class of 1997

Joy is finally figuring out how to play the VCR all by myself. I can even record.

Peach Cobbler

3 cups sliced fresh 1 cup Bisquick
   peaches 1 egg, slightly beaten
1 teaspoon lemon juice 1 cup granulated sugar
½ teaspoon nutmeg ½ stick butter, melted
½ teaspoon cinnamon

Place peaches in buttered oven-proof baking dish. Sprinkle with lemon juice, cinnamon and nutmeg. Beat egg. Add Bisquick and sugar. Stir until coarse in texture. Spread evenly over peaches. Pour butter evenly over flour mixture. Bake uncovered at 350 degrees for 45 minutes.

Wanda Hogg, Class of 1995

Cookies

In LIFE class I learned to love me. I learned that this is the first step to empowerment. I am worthy no matter what my age.

Dear Mrs. Ciaramitaro

I do not know how to tell a story of no place like home because there is no place like home. You can go any place you would like to go but there is something about returning home that makes you glad. And you say, "I am so glad to be back home." It is just a place where you feel good, and you can pull off your shoes and get comfortable and start to do what makes you feel good. And it can be so simple as taking a good old hot bath or read, or sew, or cook or go out and gather the things from your garden. It can be flowers or other things you have growing in your garden.

And there is the other side of just being at home. You can reach for all of your things you have to help with those old pains you have. Or you can just be lazy and relax and do nothing.

You just cannot beat being at home even if you are not able to get up and do what you used to, you can just look around you and smile — thinking about what was said and done at home. Or look at pictures of children and grandchildren and old friends.

I enjoy just sitting on the outside looking at the world around me. There are people who enjoy everything about being at home. I just cannot express how good it feels to be at home. Be it ever so humble, there is just not any place like being at home. Everyone knows where home is.

This is how I view home. I do hope I can stay at home until I have to go to my heavenly home.

Minnie E. Smith
LIFE Classes 92 and 2000
Memphis, Tennessee

Hello Dollies

1 stick butter, melted	1 cup chocolate or
1½ cups graham cracker	butterscotch morsels
crumbs	1½ cups flaked coconut
1 cup walnuts or pecans	1½ cups sweetened
	condensed milk

Pour melted butter into bottom of 13 x 9 inch pans. Sprinkle crumbs evenly over butter. Next add layer of chopped nuts, then chocolate morsels then coconut. Pour milk evenly over coconut layer. Bake at 350 degrees for 25 minutes or until lightly brown on top. Cool in pan for 15 minutes before cutting.

Frankie Bodden, Class of 1995

Working in a health care environment can sometimes be stressful. The employees can develop low morale at times and we found it necessary to take action to cope with the situation. Someone came up with the idea of having what was termed "togetherness". It was suggested that staff members bring their favorite food and we would eat together and vent. One staff member brought Hello Dollies and they were delicious. As we would eat them up we would release our stress and our morale would go up, up, up!

"I love to walk and hope that five years from now I will continue to be able to walk. I want to be able to work in my flower garden and also I hope that I will have a new car. And I would like to travel to Africa."

Edna Burton, Class of 1997

Rich Butter Cookies

1 cup butter	2½ cups all-purpose flour
1½ cups granulated sugar	1 teaspoon baking soda
1 egg	1 teaspoon cream of tartar
1 teaspoon vanilla	¼ teaspoon salt

Cream butter. Add sugar gradually, creaming until fluffy. Add unbeaten egg and vanilla. Beat well. Sift together dry ingredients. Blend with cream mixture. Drop by teaspoons onto ungreased cookie sheet. Bake at 375 degrees for 8 minutes.

Yield: approximately 5 dozen

Bettye Lott, Class of 1992

Boiled Cookies

2 cups granulated sugar	2 cups uncooked oats
¼ cup cocoa	1½ teaspoons vanilla
¼ cup butter	1 cup chopped nuts or
½ cup milk	coconut
⅔ cup peanut butter	

Bring sugar, cocoa, butter and milk to a boil. Remove from heat and add peanut butter. Mix until melted. Add oats and vanilla. Mix. Add nuts. Beat until thick. Pour into an 8 x 10 x 2 inch pan and cut in squares.

Thelma Glasco, Class of 1995

Joy is the bride dancing with her grandfather at the wedding reception.

I worked as a medical clerk in a dental clinic at the Veteran Affairs (V.A.) Hospital. Many of the vets would come in pretty regularly and I got to know the families. Many patients and family would bring food for the staff especially people from rural areas who brought fresh vegetables and other knick-knacks. This recipe for boiled cookies was passed on to me by a sweet senior lady who brought her husband to the V.A. clinic. I thought the idea of boiled cookies was unique and they were very good.

Cornmeal Cookies

¾ cup margarine	¼ teaspoon salt
¾ cup granulated sugar	½ cup cornmeal
1 egg	½ teaspoon nutmeg,
1½ cups all-purpose flour	optional
1 teaspoon baking powder	½ cup raisins, optional

In a large bowl, combine margarine and sugar. Add egg. Beat well. Add remaining ingredients. Mix well. Drop by teaspoon full on greased baking pan. Bake at 350 degrees for 15 minutes, or until lightly browned.

Yield: 3 dozen

Louise Fowler, Friend of Senior Leaders

Deluxe Oatmeal Raisin Cookies

1¼ cups all-purpose flour	2 eggs
1 teaspoon baking soda	1 teaspoon vanilla
½ teaspoon salt	3 cups quick oats
¾ teaspoon ground cinnamon	1 (10 ounce) package semisweet chocolate covered raisins
1 cup butter	1 cup chopped nuts
¾ cup granulated sugar	
¾ cup brown sugar	

Preheat oven to 375 degrees. Mix flour, baking soda, salt and cinnamon. In a separate bowl, combine butter, sugars, eggs and vanilla. Blend until creamy. Gradually add in flour mixture. Stir in oats, raisins and nuts. Drop onto ungreased cookie sheet. Bake for 6 minutes. Cool on rack.

B.J. Glass, Class of 1996

"If we think that we are to the point where we can't make decisions, we may just need more information. It is a wild world out there, but we can find a reputable agent. We can find the information we need."

LIFE Graduate

Poor Man's Cookies

2 cups quick rolled oats	1 teaspoon baking soda
1 cup packed brown sugar	¼ cup hot water
½ cup granulated sugar	½ cup melted and cooled shortening
1 cup all-purpose flour	1 teaspoon vanilla
¼ teaspoon salt	

Combine oats, sugars, flour and salt. Combine baking soda and water. Mix into oats. Add shortening and vanilla. Roll into walnut size balls. Place on greased cookie sheet. Bake at 350 degrees for 10 minutes or until golden brown. Remove from oven. Let stand 2 minutes before transferring to cooling rack.

Yield: 3½ dozen

Georgia Bartosch, Class of 1992

Forgotten Cookies

2	egg whites	¼	teaspoon salt
¾	cup granulated sugar	½	cup chopped nuts
1	teaspoon vanilla	1	package chocolate chips

Preheat oven to 350 degrees. Beat egg whites until stiff. Gradually add sugar and continue beating. Add vanilla, salt, nuts and chocolate chips. Drop by teaspoons onto greased and floured cookie sheet. Place in oven. Count slowly to 30 and turn off oven. Leave cookies in oven overnight. These are best if eaten within 2 days.

Eileen Stephenson, Class of 1993

Every time I leave my doctor he says, "You know what they say, if you don't use it you'll lose it."

Garden Oatmeal Raisin Cookies

½	cup non-dairy butter	1½	teaspoons cinnamon
1¾	cups oats	½	teaspoon salt
1	cup whole wheat flour	1	teaspoon baking soda
⅔	cup maple syrup	½	cup raisins
1	over-ripened banana	½	cup nuts
½	teaspoon vanilla		

Preheat oven to 375 degrees. In medium sized mixing bowl, blend banana until smooth. Add maple syrup, vanilla and butter. Blend well. In a separate bowl, sift together flour, salt and baking powder. Stir oats into dry mixture. Add dry ingredients to wet ingredients. Stir well. Add raisins and nuts. Drop by spoonfuls onto greased cookie sheet. Bake for 8 to 14 minutes or until cookies are golden brown around edges.

Josie Buckner, Class of 1992

For those of us who love sweets and are concerned about our health, this recipe offers a welcome alternative.

Chocolate Peanut Butter Oatmeal Cookies

1	cup granulated sugar	¼	cup peanut butter
¼	cup cocoa	½	teaspoon vanilla
¼	cup milk	1½	cups quick oats
½	stick butter		

Blend together sugar, cocoa, milk and butter for 1 minute. Add peanut butter, vanilla and oats. Drop teaspoon sized cookies onto waxed paper. Serve.

Georgia Bartosch, Class of 1992

Whenever cookies were needed for PTA or church these cookies were ideal to make. They do not need to be baked so they could be tossed together at last minute because most of the ingredients were kept on hand.

"I hope I will be able to continue to see and read five years from now. I want to be independent in my home and be able to walk to church, to garden, and to travel."

Marjorie Cowser, Class of 1999

Buttermilk Teacakes

1	cup butter, softened	5	cups self-rising flour
2	cups granulated sugar	¼	teaspoon baking soda
3	eggs	1	teaspoon vanilla
2	tablespoons buttermilk	½	cup granulated sugar

Cream butter. Gradually add sugar. Beat well. Add eggs, one at a time, beating well after each addition. Add buttermilk and beat well. Combine flour and baking soda. Gradually stir into cream mixture. Add vanilla and stir. Chill dough in refrigerator for 1 hour or more. Roll dough to ¼ inch thickness on a lightly floured surface. Cut with biscuit cutter. Place 1 inch apart on lightly greased cookie sheets. Sprinkle with sugar. Bake at 350 degrees for 8 minutes, or until edges are light brown. Transfer to cooling rack.

Yield: 4 dozen

Marilyn Baugus, Class of 1992

Chinese Fortune Cookies

¼ cup plus 2 tablespoons butter, softened	2 egg whites
¼ cup plus 2 tablespoons granulated sugar	½ teaspoon almond extract
	⅔ cup all-purpose flour

Grease and flour 3 cookie sheets. Draw 3 inch circles, 1 inch apart, on floured cookie sheets with tip of dull knife. Set aside. Combine first 4 ingredients. Beat at medium speed with electric mixer until blended. Stir in flour. Drop by rounded tablespoons into circles on prepared cookie sheets. Spread to fill each circle. Bake at 400 degrees for 4 minutes until edges are lightly burned. Remove from oven. Working quickly, loosen cookies with spatula, leaving on warm cookie sheet. One at a time, place folded fortunes in center of cookies. Gently fold cookie in half. Bend folded edge of cookie downward. Place in a muffin pan to harden. Repeat with remaining cookies. If cookies are cool and become too brittle to fold, return to warm oven briefly to soften.

Yield: 2½ dozen

Betty Ball, Class of 1994

Blond Brownies

¾ cup butter	1½ teaspoons vanilla
2⅓ cups light brown sugar	1 cup semisweet chocolate morsels
3 eggs	1 cup chopped nuts
2¾ cups all-purpose flour	
2½ teaspoons baking powder	

Preheat oven to 350 degrees. Grease a 13 x 9 inch baking pan. In a medium-sized saucepan, melt butter over low heat. Remove from heat and stir in brown sugar until blended. Add eggs, one at a time, blending after each addition. Add flour, baking powder and vanilla. Mix well. Stir in chocolate morsels and nuts. Pour into prepared pan. Bake for 20 to 30 minutes or until golden brown and firm to touch. Cool completely before cutting.

Betty Thompson, Class of 1994

Mama's Tea Cakes

3	cups granulated sugar	3	eggs
1	cup shortening	½	teaspoon salt
1	teaspoon baking soda	1	teaspoon nutmeg
1	cup buttermilk	4	cups all-purpose flour

Cream sugar and shortening in a bowl. Dissolve soda in buttermilk. Stir into creamed mixture. Beat in eggs, one at a time, mixing well after each addition. Stir in remaining ingredients. Mix into a soft dough. Roll out on a floured board. Cut with cookie cutter. Place on greased cookie sheet. Bake at 350 degrees for 12 to 15 minutes or until golden brown.

Yield: 48 cookies

Lillie Glover Nelson, Class of 1992

Mama cooked a large batch of these cookies when I was a young girl. Everyone would sit around the heater on a cold evening and have family news and prayer. An impromptu program was often held such as singing, praying and reciting poetry, and sometimes they were made up on the spot. All of us were show-offs and we were encouraged by our parents. The Glover clan consisted of 13 children plus Mama and Dad, and any child in the neighborhood who could get permission.

Pineapple-Cheese Breakfast Bars

1½ cups rolled oats	½ cup packed brown sugar
1 cup all-purpose flour	¾ cup pineapple preserves
1 cup granulated sugar	⅓ cup granulated sugar
1 cup flaked coconut	1 egg
1 cup chopped pecans	1 (8 ounce) package cream
¾ cup margarine, softened	cheese, softened

Preheat oven to 350 degrees. Mix oats, flour, sugar, coconut, pecans, margarine and brown sugar until crumbly. Reserve 1½ cups and set aside. Pat remaining crumbly mixture in an ungreased 13 x 9 x 2 inch pan. Bake 15 minutes. Cool 5 minutes. Spread with preserves. Mix sugar, egg and cream cheese. Pour over preserves. Sprinkle with reserved crumbly mixture. Bake 20 to 25 minutes or until top is golden brown. Cool. Cut into 2 x 1½ inch bars.

L. Almarita Johnson, Class of 1993

Texas Gold Bars

1 package yellow cake mix	1 pound confectioners' sugar
1 egg, slightly beaten	2 eggs, slightly beaten
½ cup margarine, melted	1 tablespoon vanilla
1 (8 ounce) package cream cheese	

Preheat oven to 325 degrees. Combine cake mix, egg and margarine. Press into ungreased 9 x 13 inch Pyrex pan. Do not use metal pan. Mix remaining ingredients and spread over cake mix layer. Bake at 325 degrees for 50 minutes. Allow to cool before cutting into bars.

Evelyn Cornelius, Class of 1993

Candy

*The one thing I never want
to give up is my independence.*

Keep on Going

"Truthfully, I don't know what keeps me going. I just have the desire to keep going. Therefore, I work at it. You asked me about my health. I can't see. I know you are there, but if I really wanted to see you, I would put these glasses on. Like a lot of new things, they turn dark in the light and I despise that. And I can't hear. Those are two infirmities that I started to say I suffer with. I don't suffer with, I experience them. I have high blood pressure. I'm a diabetic. I have had two surgeries. I am four disks short in the back. My cholesterol is out of sight and I've got athletes foot. But, if I decided to quit because of any of those things, that would not make it any better. And it's kind of like Dear Abby told somebody. They wrote to her and said, 'I always wanted to study medicine, but I'm 50 years old and when I get out of medical school, I will be almost 60.' And Abby wrote back and said, 'If you don't go to medical school, how old will you be in 10 years?' So, if I've got these things and I don't go on, they are not going to get any better. I'll still be just as old in a couple of years as I would be if I worried about them."

John Long
Senior Voices Participant

Martha and Nick's Family Fudge

This has been "our" fudge for over 50 years.

½ pound butter
12 ounces semi-sweet
    chocolate chips
2 teaspoons vanilla
5 ounces marshmallow
    creme

1½ cups chopped walnuts
4½ cups granulated sugar
1 (13 ounce) can
    evaporated milk

In a large heat resistant bowl, place butter, chocolate chips, vanilla, marshmallow creme and chopped walnuts. In saucepan, combine sugar and evaporated milk. Cook, stirring constantly, until it comes to a rolling boil. Start timing and cook for 7 minutes longer. Slowly pour hot mixture over ingredients in bowl. With an electric mixer, beat on high speed until smooth and creamy.

Pour on to buttered 11 x 17 inch cookie sheet. If desired, carefully place walnuts one inch apart to decorate the fudge. Cool and cut into 1 inch squares.

Martha Nichols, Friend of Senior Leaders

We have been making this fudge every year around Christmas for over 50 years. Each year we make several batches and share them with family and friends. The tins we send them out in often come back to be filled the next year. It was always Nick's job to place the walnuts on the fudge for decoration. He was the only one in the family with the patience to add this loving touch.

Never Fails Fudge

2	cups granulated sugar		Dash of salt
⅔	cup evaporated skimmed milk	1	cup semisweet chocolate pieces
12	regular marshmallows	1	cup nuts, chopped
½	cup butter	1	teaspoon vanilla

Mix sugar, milk, marshmallows, butter and salt in a heavy 2-quart saucepan. Cook, stirring constantly, over medium heat to boiling. Boil and stir 5 minutes. Remove from heat. Add chocolate pieces, stirring until completely melted. Stir in nuts and vanilla. Spread into buttered 8 inch square pan. Cool.

Yield: 30 pieces

Mary Lou Combes, Friend of Senior Leaders

This goes back to my childhood days. You know nearly every girl back in my younger days wanted to know how to make fudge. Well, I was one of them, and I would make it, and of course it never turned out right. It would always be too soft or too hard, but I never gave up on making fudge. So, we moved to Memphis back in 1965. One day I was sitting in a doctor's office waiting for my husband to see the doctor. When I am in a place like that, if there is something to read, I am going to do that. I picked up a magazine and started looking at it to see what I wanted to read and at once I saw this recipe on fudge. I didn't copy it down; I tore it right out of the magazine and took it home. I couldn't wait until I tried this recipe. Well, it didn't turn out too good. I looked at the recipe again and discovered I had cooked it two minutes too long. The next day I tried it again and it turned out good! From that day on I never had another problem making good fudge. All of my family and friends, near the holidays, begin to ask me "When are you going to start making your fudge?" This recipe became my specialty.

No Cook Divinity

1	(7.2 ounce) package fluffy white frosting mix	½ cup boiling water
⅓	cup light corn syrup	4½ cups confectioners' sugar
1	teaspoon vanilla	1 cup chopped nuts

In a small bowl, beat frosting mix, corn syrup, vanilla and boiling water with electric mixer on high speed until stiff peaks form, about 5 minutes. Transfer to large bowl. Gradually beat in sugar on low speed. Stir in nuts. Drop mixture by teaspoonfuls onto waxed paper. When outside of candy feels firm, turn over if necessary to dry bottoms. Let dry at least 12 hours. Store in airtight container.

Note: For mints, substitute ½ teaspoon peppermint extract for vanilla and 1 crushed peppermint candy for nuts.

Yield: 5½ dozen

Marilyn Baugus, Class of 1992

"In LIFE class, I got the power to be forthright and approach people that I usually wouldn't approach and say what it is I need to say."

Eloise Curtis, Class of 1994

Divinity

1	pint jar marshmallow cream	⅓ cup water
1½	cups granulated sugar	½ teaspoon vanilla
	Pinch of salt	½ cup chopped nuts

Empty marshmallow cream into large bowl, set aside. In heavy pot, mix sugar, salt and water. Bring to boil and cook until forms a hard ball when dropped into cold water. Stir hot mixture into marshmallow cream. Add vanilla and nuts. Continue stirring until slightly stiff. Drop by teaspoon full onto wax paper.

Annie McDaniel, Friend of Senior Leaders

Heavenly Cream Cheese Mints

1	(8 ounce) package cream cheese	2	pounds confectioners' sugar
	Food coloring of choice		Granulated sugar
½	ounce mint flavor		Pecans

In mixing bowl, combine cream cheese, food coloring and mint. Add confectioners' sugar, 1 pound at a time. When mixture becomes thick, but not sticky, shape into small balls or squares and roll in granulated sugar. Press pecans into center of cream cheese mixture. Let dry at least 24 hours.

Geneva Burns, Class of 1996

This is always looked forward to at Senior Leaders' annual Open House celebration.

Irish Potato Candy

1	cup mashed potatoes, cold	1½	cups smooth peanut butter
½	stick butter	1½	cups pecans, chopped
1	(1 pound) box confectioners' sugar	1	medium bottle maraschino cherries, chopped

Work butter and sugar together with potatoes, saving enough sugar to flour board. Shape in roll, place on board or pastry cloth. Roll out ¼ inch thick. Spread with complete coat of peanut butter. Sprinkle pecans and cherries over entire surface. Roll up in long roll. Wrap in waxed paper and then a lightly damp cloth. Refrigerate. When thoroughly chilled, unroll and slice ¼ inch thick.

Nelly Galloway Shearer, Friend of Senior Leaders

This recipe of my mother, Mildred Hale Galloway, was a favorite of my childhood. This was one of our "Christmas treats."

Strawberry Candy

4	small packages strawberry jello	¾	cup vegetable oil
2	cups Angel Flake coconut	1	cup evaporated milk Granulated sugar, colored red
2	cups pecans, ground		Mint or other leaves

"Please do not stereotype us. We are all different."

Mix first five ingredients. Shape into strawberries. Roll in red colored sugar. Put green leaves on.

Note: Do not make too large, as these are more attractive in smaller size.

Yield: approximately 100

Nelly Galloway Shearer, Friend of Senior Leaders

This is an attractive candy to display for tea, dessert party or other special occasion. I first used this for an Open House for my parent's 90th birthday!

Almond Butter Crunch

½	cup butter, do not use substitute	½	cup granulated sugar
2	tablespoons light corn syrup	1	cup blanched shredded almonds

Line bottom and sides of an 8 inch pan with aluminum foil. Butter foil and set aside. In a heavy skillet, melt butter. Add corn syrup, sugar and almonds. Bring to a boil over medium heat, stirring constantly until mixture turns golden brown, about 5 minutes. Immediately spread in prepared pan. Cool 15 minutes or until firm. Remove from pan and peel off foil. Cool thoroughly.

Yield: ¾ pound

Jennie Morring, Class of 1993

Turtles

3 whole pecan halves per turtle	1 caramel candy square per turtle
	Chocolate bark

Preheat oven to 300 degrees. On a cookie sheet, place 3 pecan halves in a windmill shape for each turtle you wish to make. Place 1 unwrapped candy square on each turtle. Place cookie sheet in oven and cook for 6 minutes.

Remove from oven. Flatten caramels with back of a buttered spoon. Cool for 5 minutes. In a saucepan, heat chocolate bark just to melting stage. Dip each turtle into chocolate mixture. Place on wax paper to cool.

Linda Nichols, Friend of Senior Leaders
Honorary Class of 1996

The neat thing about this recipe is that you can make any amount you wish from 1 turtle to several dozen. Growing up, my fondest childhood memories all revolve around knowing how much my parents loved me. On good days, sad days and even bad days, when I came home there was always unconditional love from my mama and daddy. When I was in high school, I came home one day after school and I asked my daddy, "Did you ever want a boy?" And he looked at me and said, "Why would I ever want a boy when I have you?" Even today when life's challenges hit hard, I am reassured by the love and acceptance my mama and daddy so generously gave me as I grew up. And even though daddy has passed away, I will never forget his simple answer to my question.

English Toffee Bars

1	pound box graham crackers	2	stick butter
1	cup chopped pecans	½	cup white or brown sugar

Line cookie sheet with foil. Grease with small amount of butter and arrange graham crackers to completely cover bottom. Sprinkle pecans over crackers. In a saucepan, mix butter and sugar. Boil 1 minute. Pour over crackers and nuts. Bake at 350 degrees for 10 to 12 minutes. Cool and break apart. These will keep in refrigerator for weeks.

Note: Chocolate chips can be added when crackers are removed from oven.

Beverlee Timm, Class of 1994

More Tasty Treats

We may be retired, but we are not expired.

Feelings About Home

"I feel very hopeful about the future, and staying in my own home. It would be very important for me to stay in pleasant surroundings where I'm accustomed to being in. And I worked all my life and tilled the soil and I love working in the garden, and doing things for me. I like being independent. I would just love to stay at home and I feel very confident that I could make it in my own home better than I could anyplace else. "

Biola Hicks

Baklava

PASTRY

1	package phyllo sheets	¼	cup granulated sugar
2	sticks butter, melted	2	teaspoons cinnamon
3	cups chopped pecans		

SYRUP

2	cups granulated sugar	1	tablespoon lemon juice
⅔	cup water		

Joy is a little voice
on the telephone,
"Hi grandma."

Make syrup by bringing all syrup ingredients to a boil. Let cool. Arrange phyllo sheets in 13 x 9 x 2 inch pan, one at a time. For each sheet, brush with melted butter using a pastry brush. Fold neatly on top and brush with butter again. Repeat this for first 10 sheets. Mix nuts, sugar and cinnamon together. Sprinkle on sheets, spreading evenly. Continue layering remaining sheets of phyllo. With a sharp knife, score top of pastry with diagonal lines about ½ inch deep and 1½ inches apart. Cross again diagonally to form diamond shapes. Pour remaining butter on top. Bake at 400 degrees for 10 minutes. Reduce heat to 350 degrees and bake for 30 minutes. Remove from oven and cool 10 minutes. Pour cooled syrup over pastry. Cool completely before serving.

Shoghig (Sunny) Ross, Senior Leaders Board of Directors

This recipe is a great way to make friends. I find wherever I take this delicious treat, someone always says, "This is delicious, where can I get more?"

Broiled Grapefruit

| 1 | grapefruit | 2 | tablespoons orange marmalade |

Slice grapefruit in half and then section by cutting on each side of the membranes. Spread orange marmalade over the top of grapefruit halves and place halves under broiler until brown. Delicious served hot. If marmalade is not available, honey may be used.

Lillian Neal, Class of 1995

About 35 years ago, I lived in New York and someone took me to a French restaurant. We were served broiled grapefruit as an appetizer, and I enjoyed it so much that I have been serving broiled grapefruit ever since. This can be used either as an appetizer or as a dessert.

Apple Dumplings

2	Granny Smith apples	1	cup orange juice
1	(8 count) package crescent rolls	1	stick margarine Cinnamon
1	cup granulated sugar		

Peel, core and quarter apples. Roll each quarter apple in opened crescent roll, beginning with large end. Place on lightly greased baking dish. In a saucepan, heat margarine, sugar and orange juice. Pour over apple rolls. Sprinkle with cinnamon. Bake at 350 degrees for 30 to 40 minutes.

Evelyn Cornelius, Class of 1993

Bourbon Balls

2	cups dark seedless raisins, chopped	½	pound confectioners' sugar
2	cups pecans, chopped	2	tablespoons cocoa
1	pound crushed vanilla wafers	6	ounces bourbon whiskey
		⅓	cup light corn syrup

Mix all ingredients together. Use your hands and shape into 1 inch balls. Roll in sugar. Store in an airtight container.

Note: If not eaten right away, balls will soak up the sugar. Just add more sugar and shake in container to coat.

Yield: 6 dozen

Committee

Apricot Balls

3	(6 ounce) packages dried apricots, cut into small pieces	1	cup chopped dates
		1	(14 ounce) can sweetened condensed milk
1	(14 ounce) package flaked coconut	½	cup confectioners' sugar

Combine apricots, coconut and dates in a large mixing bowl. Add condensed milk, mixing well. Shape into 1 inch balls and roll in sugar.

Yield: 9 dozen

Committee

"I have found that it is just as easy to cook meals for one as it was to cook them for four. I just modify the recipes, share food with friends (who also share back with me) and I eat more things raw — apples carrots, celery, bananas and so on. I love a beautiful table, so sometimes I set the table with candles, play soft music and pamper my taste buds with a special homemade treat."

LIFE Graduate

Ambrosia

1	(16 ounce) package of sweetened coconut or 1 coconut	2	cans full orange sections
		¼	cup orange juice
1	(15 ounce) can crushed pineapple	¼	cup granulated sugar, if using fresh coconut

If using fresh coconut, milk and grate meat. Combine coconut, pineapple and liquid, orange sections, orange juice and sugar. Orange section should be scooped out with a grapefruit spoon to avoid white membrane.

Linda Nichols, Honorary Class of 1996

Everyone in the South has an Ambrosia recipe. Each one is different and people are fiercely loyal to their own. For as long as I can remember, we have had this Ambrosia, which came from the mother of my mother's friend over 60 years ago.

Diabetic Strawberry Trifle

| 1 | quart strawberries | 1 | (family size) box sugar-free instant vanilla pudding |
| 1 | angel food cake | | Light Cool Whip |

Mash berries. Tear cake into 1 inch cubes. Prepare pudding as directed. Line bowl with layer of cake, berries and pudding. Repeat. Top with Cool Whip.

Jean Webb, Class of 1993

My cousin was diagnosed with diabetes several years ago. At that time he was left out at dessert time. His wife developed this dessert for him. She entered it in a Dairy contest for the state of Tennessee and won a blue ribbon.

Orange Slice Roll

1	(1 pound) package vanilla wafers	1	(14 ounce) can condensed milk
1	pound orange slice candy, chopped	1	cup coconut Powdered sugar
1	cup pecans, chopped		

Blend wafers in a blender or crush with a rolling pin until fine. Add candy and pecans. Stir in milk. Add coconut. Mix well. Form into two small rolls. Roll in powdered sugar. Roll up in waxed paper and foil. Chill overnight. Slice and serve.

Evelyn Cornelius, Class of 1993

Joy is a grandpa holding a little hand just right around a fishing pole.

Persimmon Pudding

½	cup margarine	½	teaspoon nutmeg
⅔	cup granulated sugar	2	cups persimmon pulp
2	eggs	2	cups buttermilk
1	teaspoon vanilla	1	cup all-purpose flour
½	teaspoon cinnamon	1	teaspoon baking soda
½	teaspoon cloves		Whipped cream

Preheat oven to 350 degrees. Cream margarine and sugar. Add eggs. Whisk with fork until smooth. Add vanilla, cinnamon, cloves, nutmeg, persimmon pulp and buttermilk. Stir until well blended. Sift in flour and baking soda. Stir until well blended. Pour into buttered 9 x 13 inch baking dish. Bake 50 minutes. Let stand about 10 minutes. Pudding will "fall" as it cools. Cut into squares and serve with whipped cream.

Note: One cup of flour will make a moist, pie-like pudding. If you like your pudding more cakey, add additional flour. Do not add more than ½ cup.

Sandra Engelhardt, Friend of Senior Leaders

I love my computer. I love the games. I love the internet. I love email. I am so grateful to have lived long enough to experience all this new technology.

Allaise Pudding

BATTER

½ cup packed brown sugar
2 teaspoons baking powder
1½ cups all-purpose flour

1 cup raisins
1 stick butter
⅛ teaspoon salt
½ cup milk

SAUCE

1½ cups packed brown sugar
1 tablespoon cornstarch

3 cups boiling water
1 tablespoon butter
1 teaspoon vanilla

Mix together ingredients for batter. In a separate bowl, mix together ingredients for sauce. Pour batter mixture into sauce. Pour into 2½-quart dishes. Bake at 325 degrees for 45 minutes. Top with whipped cream.

Helen Lockhart, Class of 1995

Brown Betty

2 cups fine bread crumbs
3 cups stewed sweetened apples

3 tablespoons butter

Melt butter. Add bread crumbs, stirring until all butter is absorbed. Grease pudding dish. Press layer of crumb mixture in bottom, then apples. Repeat layers, ending with crumb mixture. Dot with butter. Bake at 325 degrees for 45 minutes.

Helen Lockhart, Class of 1995

Banana Pudding I

1	cup granulated sugar	4	tablespoons butter
6	tablespoons all-purpose flour	1	teaspoon vanilla
		5	ounces vanilla wafers
¾	teaspoon salt	6	large ripe bananas
4	eggs		Whipping cream,
4	cups milk		optional

Blend sugar, flour, salt and eggs. Beat until well mixed. Add milk. Cook over low heat until thickened, Add butter and vanilla. Arrange wafers in bottom of 2½ quart dish. Spoon ½ of mixture over wafers. Slice bananas over custard. Repeat until all ingredients are used.

Lucille Vescova, Class of 1992

Banana Pudding II

4	tablespoons all-purpose flour	½	teaspoon vanilla
		1	(1 pound) bag vanilla wafers
½	cup granulated sugar		
¼	teaspoon salt	1	pound bananas
2	cups scalded milk	¼	cup granulated sugar
2	eggs, separated		

Mix together flour, ½ cup sugar and salt in top of double boiler. Slowly stir in hot milk and cook until thickened. Stir ¼ cup hot mixture into beaten egg yolks. Pour back into double boiler. Cook 2 more minutes. Remove from heat. Add vanilla and cool until warm. In a baking dish, alternate layers of vanilla wafers, sliced bananas and pudding. Beat egg whites until foamy. Add ¼ cup sugar and beat until stiff. Pile lightly on pudding. Bake at 400 degrees for 8 minutes or until golden brown.

Maxine Crivens Ivy, Class of 1997

It was so much fun making banana pudding, but even more fun seeing and tasting the finished product. After serving the family banana pudding, the remaining would be put in the refrigerator. As a child, I would stand in the refrigerator door with a spoon and eat it straight from the baking dish. My parents would always accuse my brother of being the pudding thief, and he would be the one getting punished.

Joy is finding love again.

"Because I am 70 years old, everyone expects my favorite movie to be Casa Blanca. Hey, that movie was okay, but I like Forrest Gump, Gladiator and some of those space movies. I don't buy that line that all the good stuff happened in the past."

LIFE Graduate

Bread Pudding

"The things we are doing now are for the young as well as for seniors."

½	cup golden raisins		Cinnamon, optional
1	cup hot water	2	cups milk or half-and-half
5	slices day-old white bread, crusts removed	½	cup granulated sugar
3	tablespoons butter, softened	1	teaspoon vanilla
		2	eggs

Preheat oven to 350 degrees. Soak raisins in hot water for 5 minutes. Drain. Spread one side of each bread slice with butter. Cut slices in half. Place in 8 inch square baking dish buttered side up. Sprinkle raisins and cinnamon over bread. Heat milk and sugar until steaming. Remove from heat and stir in vanilla. In a separate bowl, beat eggs lightly. Gradually stir in hot milk mixture. Pour over bread. Bake, uncovered, for 30 minutes or until golden brown.

Yield: 4 servings

Betty Thompson, Class of 1995

For me, bread pudding is a comforting, pampering kind of food. I have a friend who knows of my love for this simple dessert. And from time to time, she will send me a recipe she has found and tried. She adds her comments and any changes she's made in preparing the dish. Then I make it and make my own changes or additions. This is one of those recipes. It is very tasty, satisfying and easy!

Glover Family Old-Fashioned Bread Pudding with Lemon Butter Sauce

PUDDING

4	cups toasted bread crumbs	½	cup granulated sugar
½	cup seedless raisins, optional	½	teaspoon salt
		1	teaspoon cinnamon
2	large cans evaporated milk	1	stick butter
		½	teaspoon nutmeg
4	eggs, beaten	1	teaspoon vanilla extract

SAUCE

2	tablespoons butter	½	cup lemon juice
1	cup granulated sugar		Grated lemon rind
2	eggs, beaten		

Combine bread crumbs and raisins. Press into 2½ quart baking dish. Mix milk, eggs, sugar, salt, cinnamon, ½ stick of butter, nutmeg and vanilla. Beat with mixer until thoroughly blended. Pour over bread and raisin. Dot with remaining butter. Bake at 350 degrees for 1 hour. In a bowl, cream butter. Gradually add sugar. Blend. Add eggs, lemon juice and lemon rind. Transfer to double boiler and heat until thick. Pour over hot pudding. Serve warm or chilled.

Yield: 8 to 10 servings

Lillie Glover Nelson, Class of 1992

In LIFE class, I learned not to define myself as an old person, or a diabetic, or needy person. I learned to define myself as who I know myself to me. I'm a free spirit. I'm loosing my cocoon of all those labels.

Gajjar Halwa
Gold Crush/Carrot Halwa

> "I accepted the fact that I was a member of the senior population and I didn't need to be ashamed. In fact, I am proud of my age."
>
> *Elizabeth Burns, Class of 1994*

1	cup melted shortening or oil	1	cup non-fat dry milk powder
4	cups carrots, grated	8	whole cardamom, peeled and crushed
1	cup half-and-half		
1	cup milk	½	cup slivered almonds and pistachios
1	cup granulated sugar		

In a 4 quart pan, melt shortening over low heat. Stir in carrots and sauté until light medium brown. Add half-and-half, milk and sugar, stirring continually. Add dry milk powder slowly and stir evenly. Add cardamom. Continue cooking on low to medium heat until mixture reaches consistency of thick pie filling. Stir in 2 tablespoons almonds and pistachios. Use remaining almonds and pistachios to garnish.

Asan Tejwani, Senior Leaders Board of Directors

Apple Rings

6	pounds firm, tart apples	¼	teaspoon red food coloring, more if desired
4	cups water		
4	cups granulated sugar		
1½	tablespoons ground cinnamon		

Core apples and slice into ¼ inch rings. Drop rings into lemon juice. Soak 20 minutes. Combine remaining ingredients in Dutch oven and bring to boil. Remove syrup from heat. Drain apple rings. Add to syrup. Let stand 10 minutes. Return apple mixture to heat and simmer, uncovered, 20 minutes stirring occasionally. Remove from heat and cool slightly. Weigh down apples in syrup. Let stand overnight to absorb food coloring.

Dorothy Conyers, Class of 2000

Beverages

I'm Fine

"To me hooking rugs is therapy. I think it is something that keeps my mind occupied and I feel now I want to get this done and I keep thinking positive that I will get this done. And it goes through my mind that without something like this I would be dormant just like a lot of these other gals that think at 80 years old you are old and sitting still and they are going to get old, but they are going to get like a vegetable. You got to keep going. You got to keep your hands going. Like the Doctor told me, 'Carmen use that hand. I know it hurts you every time you pick something up, but let it hurt. It is better to let it hurt than to let it get so you will never be able to use it. And that is what it will do if you don't keep active.' So I think that is the best therapy you can get. If you sit it you become stagnant. And I haven't got to that point yet. I like doing this and I would like to do another one if the Lord lets me live long enough. And the river don't rise, you got to watch out for that old river here in Arkansas.

Carmen Rutherford, age 93
Senior Voices Participant

Tomato Juice Cocktail

1 (64 ounce) can tomato juice
½ bell pepper, sliced
½ onion, sliced
1 stalk celery with leaves

½ lemon, sliced
Pinch of salt
Worcestershire sauce to taste

Joy is a wheelchair ramp into your friend's home.

Mix together all ingredients and chill.

Thelda Stevenson, Class of 1995

This cocktail was served with Triscuit crackers each month before the business women's meeting. Mrs. Withers, the church hostess, would have it ready for the ladies as they arrived before the dinner hour. This was several years ago. I still serve this at home after Christmas Eve service while getting other refreshments ready for my family and guests.

Sparkling Champagne Punch

2 cups cranberry juice cocktail
2 cups orange juice
¼ cup lemon juice

½ cup sugar
1½ cups white wine, chilled
1 bottle champagne, chilled

Combine cranberry juice cocktail, orange juice, lemon juice and sugar in a bowl, stirring until the sugar dissolves. Chill in refrigerator. Stir in wine and champagne before serving.

Terry Adams, Friend of Senior Leaders

"We like to laugh and have fun like anyone else."

Kahlúa-Under-The-Sink

3½ cups granulated sugar	5 tablespoons instant coffee
1 vanilla bean, at least 3 inches long	1 quart vodka

Dissolve sugar in 1 pint of water. Add vanilla bean and boil slowly for 30 minutes. Dissolve instant coffee in ¼ cup of boiling water. Blend coffee mix in a ½ gallon bottle containing vodka. Add sugar-water slowly. Let stand for two weeks (if you can).

It helps to hide the bottle under the sink or somewhere you won't see it!

Note: This delicious drink may be added to coffee, and is great over ice cream. Happy Sipping!

Yield: 1½ quarts

Evelyn Cornelius, Class of 1993

This recipe came from an artist friend who studied in Europe and Mexico before she married and moved to Albuquerque, New Mexico. It was while living there that she acquired this recipe. This is one of many good recipes she has passed along to me. We enjoy making and sipping Kahlúa-Under-The-Sink now that she is a resident of Memphis.

My Favorite Punch

1	(46 ounce) can red Hawaiian punch	½ gallon vanilla ice cream
1	(46 ounce) can pineapple juice	½ gallon pineapple sherbet

Mix all ingredients together and serve.

Yield: 40 cups

Committee

"I have gained knowledge to use in talking with government officials and I have brought about changes. With that knowledge, overall I learned about new opportunities."

Bertha Brasfield, Class of 1994

Instant Russian Tea

½	cup Tang	¼ teaspoon ground cinnamon
⅓	cup instant tea	⅛ teaspoon cloves
¼	cup granulated sugar	
3	tablespoons pre-sweetened lemonade mix	

Mix together ingredients. Add 8 cups of boiling water and serve hot. For individual servings, add 2 to 3 teaspoons of tea mix to 8 ounces of hot water. Store unused tea mix in airtight container.

Note: Russian Tea was very popular in the 1970s and early 1980s much like cappuccino is today.

Margaret Ann Houston, Class of 1995

Christmas Punch I

2	small packages red or green jello	3	cups canned orange juice
3½	cups granulated sugar	2	(46 ounce) cans pineapple juice
10	cups hot water	1	quart ginger ale chilled
4	(6 ounce) cans frozen lemonade		

Dissolve jello and sugar in hot water. Cool. Add juices. Chill. Add ginger ale just before serving.

Merle Smith, Class of 1998

Christmas Punch II

1	pint weak tea	4	cups cranberry juice
1	cup undiluted lemon juice	6	cups pineapple juice
1	(6 ounce) can frozen orange juice plus 2 cans of water	1	scant cup granulated sugar
		1	quart ginger ale
			Maraschino cherries

Mix tea and juices with sugar and pour over ice. Add ginger ale and cherries.

Yield: 40 cups

Committee

Christmas Wassail

1	quart hot tea	¾	cup lemon juice
1	quart cranberry juice	12	whole cloves
1	quart apple juice	3	(2 inch) cinnamon sticks
2	cups orange juice	1	orange, sliced
1	cup granulated sugar	1	lemon, sliced

Combine all ingredients, except orange and lemon slices, and heat to just below boiling. Pour into punch bowl and float lemon and orange slices.

Yield: 20 servings

Anne Weathers, Class of 1995

I don't like change. One day I realized how good I am at dealing with change. I decided to celebrate this about myself. My best friend and I went to the ice cream shop and shared a banana split. We had fun reviewing all the changes we had survived in our life and what we had learned from them.

Char

½   pint milk   Sugar to taste, optional
1   teaspoon fresh tea
    leaves, or 1 tea bag

Boil milk. Place tea leaves in a heated pot and add the boiled milk. Steep for 7 minutes. Serve immediately. Add sugar to taste.

Note: For Boiled Char, place all ingredients in a sauce pan and let barely simmer for about 5 minutes. This tea has a biting flavor of tannin and is exceptionally good.

Yield: 1 serving

Jennie Morring, Class of 1993

Joy is holding hands with your husband at the baptism of your first grandchild.

Coffee Slush

¼   cup half-and-half   Dash of cloves, optional
1½ teaspoons instant coffee   2   cups crushed ice
2   tablespoons granulated
    sugar

Blend half-and-half and coffee in a blender on high until coffee is dissolved. Add sugar and cloves. Add crushed ice ½ cup at a time, blending thoroughly after each addition. Serve immediately in chilled glasses.

Yield: 2 servings

Committee

Fruit Smoothie

2	cups frozen mixed berries	1	(8 ounce) container fruit yogurt
1	medium banana	½	cup orange juice

Blend ingredients in a blender at medium speed just until smooth and well blended.

Yield: 2 servings

Heather Baugus, Honorary Class of 1998

"Get out of your bed, do your walking, get in the bed, get your sleep, drink more water, eat more fruit, you'll be surprised what happens."

Dick Gregory
Actor, Activist, Athlete and Comedian
Participant,
Senior Voices Project

Quick Boiled Custard

1	can Eagle Brand milk	2	(3 ounce) packages instant pudding mix
¼	cup granulated sugar	½	gallon milk

In a blender, blend first 3 ingredients. Add milk almost to top of blender. Pour mixture into pitcher. Add remaining milk. Refrigerate 2 hours before serving.

Yield: 3 quarts

Marilyn Baugus, Class of 1992

Cafe Mocha

The sun setting is no less beautiful than the sun rising…

2	ounces fresh espresso	1¼	cups milk or half-and-half, steamed
3	tablespoons Gharidelli Chocolate and Cocoa Powder		Whipped cream, optional
½	tablespoon brown sugar		Cinnamon, optional

In a mug, drop in cocoa powder and brown sugar. Stir in hot espresso. Add steamed milk, stir. Top with whipped cream. Sprinkle with cinnamon if desired.

Heather Baugus, Honorary Class of 1998

Pass It On

Memories not cherished are memories that perish.

Special Recipes and Memories

This section is for you. Share your special recipes and memories from your kitchen table with those you love, and pass this cookbook on to them.

Pass It On _____

_____

_____

_____

_____

_____

_____

_____

_____

_____

_____

_____

_____

_____

_____

_____

_____

_____

_____

_____

_____

_____

_____

_____

Pass It On

Pass It On

Pass It On

Pass It On

Index

Senior Leaders Cookbook

Recipes and Memories from our Kitchen Table to Yours

2670 Union Avenue Extended, Suite 1000
Memphis, TN 38112
(901) 324-3299

Please send _____ copy(ies)   @ $19.95 each $_____

Postage and handling (First book)   @ $ 3.50 each $_____

Postage and handling for each
    additional book to same address   @ $ 1.50 each $_____

Taxes (Tennessee residents pay 8.25% sales tax)   @ $ 1.65 each $_____

                                           TOTAL $_____

Name _____

Address _____

City _____ State _____ Zip _____

Phone _____

Payment: ❑ Check   ❑ Visa   ❑ MasterCard

Card number _____ Expiration date _____

Signature _____

Make checks payable to Senior Leaders, Inc.
Thank you for supporting the programs of Senior Leaders, Inc.

- -

Senior Leaders Cookbook

Recipes and Memories from our Kitchen Table to Yours

2670 Union Avenue Extended, Suite 1000
Memphis, TN 38112
(901) 324-3299

Please send _____ copy(ies)   @ $19.95 each $_____

Postage and handling (First book)   @ $ 3.50 each $_____

Postage and handling for each
    additional book to same address   @ $ 1.50 each $_____

Taxes (Tennessee residents pay 8.25% sales tax)   @ $ 1.65 each $_____

                                           TOTAL $_____

Name _____

Address _____

City _____ State _____ Zip _____

Phone _____

Payment: ❑ Check   ❑ Visa   ❑ MasterCard

Card number _____ Expiration date _____

Signature _____

Make checks payable to Senior Leaders, Inc.

Senior Leaders Cookbook

Recipes and Memories from our Kitchen Table to Yours

2670 Union Avenue Extended, Suite 1000
Memphis, TN 38112
(901) 324-3299

Please send _____ copy(ies)	@	$19.95 each	$_____
Postage and handling (First book)	@	$ 3.50 each	$_____
Postage and handling for each additional book to same address	@	$ 1.50 each	$_____
Taxes (Tennessee residents pay 8.25% sales tax)	@	$ 1.65 each	$_____
		TOTAL	$_____

Name _____

Address _____

City _____ State _____ Zip _____

Phone _____

Payment: ❑ Check ❑ Visa ❑ MasterCard

Card number _____ Expiration date _____

Signature _____

Make checks payable to Senior Leaders, Inc.
Thank you for supporting the programs of Senior Leaders, Inc.

- -

Senior Leaders Cookbook

Recipes and Memories from our Kitchen Table to Yours

2670 Union Avenue Extended, Suite 1000
Memphis, TN 38112
(901) 324-3299

Please send _____ copy(ies)	@	$19.95 each	$_____
Postage and handling (First book)	@	$ 3.50 each	$_____
Postage and handling for each additional book to same address	@	$ 1.50 each	$_____
Taxes (Tennessee residents pay 8.25% sales tax)	@	$ 1.65 each	$_____
		TOTAL	$_____

Name _____

Address _____

City _____ State _____ Zip _____

Phone _____

Payment: ❑ Check ❑ Visa ❑ MasterCard

Card number _____ Expiration date _____

Signature _____

Make checks payable to Senior Leaders, Inc.
Thank you for supporting the programs of Senior Leaders, Inc.